The Melancholy of Rebirth

GEORGE KONRÁD

The Melancholy of Rebirth

ESSAYS FROM POST-COMMUNIST

CENTRAL EUROPE

1989–1994

Selected and Translated by Michael Henry Heim

A HELEN AND KURT WOLFF BOOK

A HARVEST ORIGINAL

HARCOURT BRACE & COMPANY

San Diego   New York   London

Library of Congress Cataloging-in-Publication Data
Konrád, György.
[Új jászületés melankóliája. English]
The melancholy of rebirth: essays from post-communist Central Europe,
1989-1994/George Konrad; translated from the Hungarian by
Michael Henry Heim.—1st ed.
p.   cm.
"A Harvest original"
ISBN 0-15-600252-3
1. Hungary—Politics and government—1989-   I. Title.
DB958.3.K6613   1996
943.905'3—dc20   94-39650

Designed by Lori J. McThomas
Printed in the United States of America
First edition
A B C D E

Contents

A Self-Introduction

K. is a fifty-seven-year-old novelist and essayist. His citizenship and native language are Hungarian, his religion Jewish. His father owned a hardware shop in the provinces; his mother is alive and well. He has four children by two marriages. He is by training a teacher of literature. His wife, Judit Lakner, is a historian. He lives in a three-room-plus-study apartment in the garden suburbs of Buda and owns a run-down house in the country. His wardrobe is modest, though he has several typewriters. Sitting at his desk, he can see flowers on the balcony, a poplar farther off, and a hospital, the one where his two grown children, now in Paris, were born a quarter of a century ago. Every morning twenty-year-old Erika comes and takes his two young sons off on their adventures.

He had a happy childhood in a house full of friends and relatives, but in 1944 he barely missed being sent to Auschwitz, where nearly all the other Jewish children from his village ended up and died. He was liberated in January 1945 in Budapest, and if the Russians had not come, he would have been shot and tossed into the Danube by the Arrow Cross, the Hungarian Fascist Party. These biographical data explain his antipathy for the extreme right.

While at secondary school he joined the students' association, but was excluded for something he wrote. He was reinstated, then excluded again. When in the summer of 1956 he received a letter telling him he was to be reinstated yet again, he failed to respond. He was expelled several times from the University for his bourgeois origins and behavior, but was finally allowed to graduate in 1956 thanks to the patronage of his instructors. He became a staff member of a new magazine, one of the voices of critical thought, for critical thought was making a comeback at the time. Its maiden issue would have appeared on 23 October 1956. That was the day the revolution broke out. K. joined the National Guard. He kept his machine gun under the bed. He never shot at anyone with it, though he did occasionally take it for a walk. His orders were to defend the University, but the Soviet troops never opened fire on it. At the time of the great exodus late in 1956 most of his friends went west; he, a family man by then, stayed put. The most obvious thing for him to do was speak and write his native language here in Hungary.

For three years after the revolution he was unemployed. Then he managed to find work as a public guardianship officer, as it was called then; it meant working with problem children and the problem adults related to them. For seven years he made the rounds of crowded tenements, coming to know virtually every kind of person living in them and to look upon the normal and the deviant in relative terms. He also took part in the young writers' subculture of the sixties. He worked part-time editing the collected works of Gogol, Turgenev, Tolstoy, and Dostoevsky, which came out in thick, leather-bound tomes on the India paper once reserved for bibles. In 1965 he was given the position of urban sociologist by an institute of town planning. Though less than qualified, he learned fast, traveling all over the country and interviewing all sorts of people. He was especially interested in the urban settlement as cultural galaxy or, if you like, as novel without end. In 1973 pressure from the secret police caused him to be dismissed from his post. He was subsequently banned from all employment and remained so for sixteen years, until 1989. He was an active member of the semilegal network of friends that called itself the democratic opposition and that emerged from the underground in 1988, on the basis of a resolution by its nearly thousand founding members under the name of the Alliance of Free Democrats. Until then he had never belonged to a party (though he had been a member of the Writers Association).

He had written essays as a young man, but was thirty-six by the time he published his first novel, *The Case Worker*. The novel owes a great deal to his experiences as a guardianship officer. It created quite a furor on the Hungarian literary scene, and was condemned and condoned. Translated into thirteen languages, it enjoyed critical acclaim abroad. For the first time in his life he received a decent royalty—and not a moment too soon: he had just been arrested with his friend and colleague Iván Szelényi, with whom he had done research in urban sociology and written a study on socialism and the intelligentsia.

Before they had time to microfilm the manuscript, which ana-
lyzed the vicissitudes of power wielded by intellectuals as a class,
the authorities ordered it destroyed. Although many labored to
carry out this noble order, the authors had kept two carbon
copies. The book eventually appeared in the West and consequently had a certain currency in Budapest as well. That was
a time when sociological studies still mattered. K.'s next novel,
The City Builder, was rejected by the publisher: Too bleak. It
therefore appeared first in the West. A censored version came
out in Budapest later, in 1977. After that K. was not heard
from at home: because his sins kept mounting and he refused
to censor himself, he fell under a total ban. During the next
twelve years he published in the independent, underground,
samizdat press, that is, for a highly discriminating audience but
one that numbered no more than a few thousand. His next two
novels, *The Loser* and *A Feast in the Garden*, first appeared in
samizdat, as did three essay collections, one of which, *Antipolitics*, was a critique of the "Yalta system" and its disastrous
consequences for the fate of Central Europe. Now that system
has come undone—to a significant extent as a result of internal
opposition. When in 1989 freedom of the press managed to
break out before the bottom fell out of the publishing industry,
five of K.'s books appeared in Budapest at once. He also began
to contribute regularly to newspapers and periodicals.

The Melancholy of Rebirth

Thoughts on the Border

*(Speech Delivered August 19, 1989 near Sopron in Celebration
of the Partial Opening of the Hungarian-Austrian Border)*

The first thing we must agree upon is that we have made up
our minds to win this end-of-the-millennium match. The Tatars
are not after us; we are not at war; there are no dreadful secrets
coming to light or tortured prisoners staggering out of prison;
no one is up in arms about anything or can point to a clear-
cut enemy. After all, we are standing here at the Iron Curtain
with the knowledge and permission of the Hungarian regime.
That regime has been vanquished from within, vanquished by
our common desire to bring down this curtain because it is a
false and evil construct and because our sense of responsibility
has grown with the recognition of our freedom to speak out.

Our historical and geographical consciousness is expanding.
A hundred years ago there were no armed guards along this
border between Austria and Hungary; there was no passport
needed to cross it. I am glad that even though we still need a
passport, we can now go back and forth as we please. This is
something we should be able to take for granted, at least in our

cultural region, the geographical center of Europe. As the walls
come tumbling down, what once seemed portentous becomes
pitiful and ludicrous; the entire structure that supported the
now crumbling Iron Curtain in public and private discourse is
crumbling in people's minds as well. When we see the heaps
of rubble, when we see the barbed wire—symbol of so many
labor camps—turning into rubbish or even marketable souve-
nirs, we feel a certain self-confidence. Yes, ladies and gentlemen, here we are, treading what was once forbidden and
forbidding ground. We have prevailed.

A thousand years ago King Stephen I made a wise decision
for this part of the globe. When the head of the Magyars—
like the heads of the Czechs, Poles, Swedes, and Danes—
accepted the norms of Western Christianity, he had trouble
teaching his sun-worshiping nomads to respect the divinity of
a Hebrew shaman nailed to a cross and to settle in one place
and work the land instead of raiding and marauding. They had
to adopt a completely new identity. But as it was a time when
a man could be dismembered for disobedience, even the most
unruly among them who might grumble, "What a bore, this
feudalism!" eventually came round and learned to live with it.
With what? Europe. Their immediate neighbors and the more
distant ones as well. They learned to look around. When they
had learned their lesson well, they fashioned a strong Hungarian
medieval kingdom; when they forgot it, their luck forsook them
and they lost their sovereignty. And once you lose your sovereignty, you lose your freedom and become a bondsman, a
vassal. Thus the Hungarian ethos combines sovereignty and
servility.

The goal in this match is to win back our sovereignty. In
a satellite state all citizens, humble or proud, are servants. Find

me an honest man in a totalitarian or even relatively liberal yet paternalistic society. You'll look long and hard. Find me a truthsayer in a society where the state is the father—state socialism, for instance —and where the man at the top has the power of a king. In a satellite state it is fitting to lie or, rather, it is impossible to know what is a lie and what is the truth. Win back our sovereignty? No, learn what sovereignty is, cultivate it, refine it, conserve it. What we need to concentrate on now is how to rid ourselves of the servile, satellite mentality so deeply ingrained in our history, in our sayings, our self-justifications, ourselves. You are a servant as long as you consider defenselessness a normal, natural condition. As long as you feel subservient, as long as you fear your superiors, as long as you are a victim rather than a team player, you have not learned sovereignty. If young Hungarians engrave in their hearts and minds those concepts of freedom that the citizens of the mature European democracies have taken generations to develop, if they not so much expect freedom as choose it and the hard work it entails, then freedom will be theirs to keep, and weapons and barbed wire mere scrap metal.

Why are we freer than we were two years ago? Why are we able to stand here? Why have we dared open our mouths? It is not to scream, no, but to put our thoughts into words, now and for the rest of our lives. Thoughts about how tired we are of paternalistic kings, of our father Franz Joseph and our father Horthy and our father Rákosi and our father Kádár! No individual can bring us salvation. Let us not then place our fate in any individual's hands. Let us not entrust total responsibility to any mother's son. The mature citizen of a mature state needs no guardian, no savior, no patriarch from on high who will rob loyal citizens of their maturity. What is happening now is perfectly normal; allusions to an emergency situation or anarchy or hysteria are out of place. To anyone who says we need a new paternalism because we are acting like dogs and require a whip to keep us in line, I say that in my experience it has always been the regime that acted like a dog: it bit when it was feared, and when it was looked straight in the eye, it retreated.

What I want to feel above me is a parliament vested with great power, not a president vested with great power. I am not partial to the Bonaparte tradition: France is a democracy in spite of Bonapartism, not because of it. Even in America (where I happened to witness last year's presidential campaign) the president must be a powerful monarch indeed if the democratic press goes into details of his private life that do not concern me in the slightest. The founders of democracies currently taking the place of dictatorships and personality-cult regimes are right to mistrust charismatic ambition and forestall it by circumscribing executive privilege. Never again do I wish to live through a period that can be stamped with the name of an individual.

We are standing on a border, so let me conclude with the following thought. There are countries you leave without showing your passport; you show it only when entering. Anyone may leave a free country. So long as our Central European confreres cannot leave their countries, so long as several hundred East German citizens with a definite destination can land in East German prison because, branded as "state serfs," they have been turned away from the border between Hungary and Austria and forced back to a homeland where *Staatsflucht*, "fleeing the state," is punishable by law—so long as that happens, we ourselves are not free. We must keep in mind that our humanity is our greatest capital. With it almost anything is possible; without it, nothing.

We are rich in anniversaries: the anniversary of the German-Soviet Nonaggression Pact, of the beginning of World War II, of the invasion of Czechoslovakia by its socialist neighbors. And let us not forget our Communist Constitution, to say nothing of the Festival of New Bread and Saint Stephen's Day fireworks over Gellért Hill. Take your pick. And what do these anniversaries tell us? Perhaps that the all-consuming nationalism of the superpowers is to the smaller nations' nationalism of self-preservation as wolf egotism is to lamb egotism. For lambs are not so meek among themselves: When there was someone to be gobbled, they have gobbled; when there was someone to be betrayed, they have betrayed.

You may accuse me of spoiling the holiday mood, but I think that only the strong are capable of looking themselves in the eye. The most important Jewish holiday of the year, Yom Kippur, is approaching. It is the Day of Atonement, the day when we give the Lord an accounting of our sins, a day of introspection and meditation. The spirit of the holiday is one of learning to look oneself in the eye, not one of collective swagger. On our own Saint Stephen's Day each of us Hungarians can take pride in having preserved our national identity against great odds. Every instance of national autonomy and solidarity among nations is cause for celebration; every instance of national bondage and treachery among nations is cause for penitence.

Every mass grave shall be opened; every confidential document shall be made public; every foul deed shall be revenged. The only criteria of behavior acceptable among nations are those acceptable among individuals in civilized society. We cannot condone the armed invasion of a neighboring country any more than we can condone the breaking and entering of a neighbor's house. In both cases the perpetrators are bandits.

We were just such bandits twenty years ago, when we jointly occupied Czechoslovakia (even if we were probably once more choosing the lesser evil). Twentieth-century history—our own, our neighbors'—has been a pretty grim business: a succession of mutual invasions with the permission of the great powers; the oppression of minorities and the near extermination of one of them (the one that gave us the book that is the base of all Christian Europe, the Bible), and this was the doing of not only the Germans. The rare cases when refugees were taken in, hidden, and saved, when individuals stood up for the victims, do provide some consolation, and we should be thankful for them. To say that it is wrong to deliver refugees to the minions of the law is a matter not of abstract principle but of elementary respect. What you do with people in distress who put their trust in you determines your fate as much as theirs. To be a friend or a traitor is a matter of self-determination.

Here in Central Europe, two hundred years after the French Revolution and the declaration of the rights due each and every individual, we can prove worthy of the epithet "European" by making ourselves allies in one another's freedom and by working towards a democratic Central European federation. For only as such can we eventually be assimilated into the alliance of West European democracies. Since we cannot escape geography, we have an extremely difficult time ahead of us. All is not hopeless, however, for we are standing here today rejoicing where only yesterday there was an Iron Curtain.

Letter from Budapest

For two weeks now the city has been downed by the heat. Flimsily dressed tourists wilt in congested traffic. You can hardly make your way along the Danube promenade in the evening: here a redheaded violinist, there a juggler, there an artist snipping silhouettes. A thin man with tattoos all over his face—after spending the last few years in jail (most recently for statutory rape), he has turned to novel writing and is on his way to fame—is giving an interview to a Scandinavian reporter, her eyes radiating fascination and sympathy.

Four hundred new private publishers are on the lookout for sensation. Censorship is a thing of the past. My books are available not only in bookshops but also on tables in the streets, side by side with pulp, politics, and religion—all previously taboo. The only films playing are American: once the temperature rises, audiences have no use for our gloomy Hungarian offerings. State-sponsored filmmaking is on its way out; I have seen the harvest of its final year. Art in general has broken with the regime. The state that pays and punishes is crumbling. Studios and editorial boards alike have pushed out from the haven of state subsidy to the free market's open sea.

One poll says the Communist Party would still win ten percent of the vote, another says twenty. Not enough to form a government. I meet a Party functionary who claims that a third of his colleagues have switched jobs. The younger, better trained among them leave—they can find work in their fields —while the older and less educated tend to stay put. The Party's potential voters are likewise older and less educated; moreover, they are likely to come from rural areas. "Parachuting," a process whereby Party officials move into private enterprise at astronomically high salaries, is all the rage and has the parachuters' colleagues furious. The Communist Party is gradually being absorbed by private enterprise, and the political elite occupies a privileged position on the privatization ladder—nearer the fire, so to speak. In any case, the turnover from functionary to entrepreneur is rampant.

From the copious literature on 1956, 1968, and 1981 (the documentation of revenge) many have learned that a flush of freedom is followed by a rush of tanks. But the army has cut its ties with the Party, the police has begun to pull in its horns, members of the paramilitary Party corps known as the Workers' Militia have suggested to the comrades that it has no place in a constitutional democracy and might as well be disbanded, and the *nomenklatura* no longer makes use of its right to bear arms. Still, a number of leaders of the Alliance of Free Democrats have received letters and calls with the message "You will hang!" If Stalinism can no longer count on votes, it still has its militant followers.

The change in regime has been a boon for people who enjoy passing judgment, and some have made an amazingly speedy transition from communist moralizing to anticommunist moralizing. The nationalist, traditionalist first-person plural mode of speech will probably have an easier time taking over the state socialist first-person plural than will the liberal "This is what I think." The red-white-and-green tricolor is replacing its all-red predecessor. Meanwhile, the parliamentary playing field is being divided up among the standard spiritual-political teams: instead of the former statist vs. civil or communist vs. anticommunist duality we have the West European lineup of national and Christian-democrat conservative liberals on one side and liberals and social democrats on the other. The reform communists are oscillating between a populist and a liberal rhetoric and may eventually have something original to contribute. Liberal democrats do not wish to exclude anyone from the game; they just want to make sure it is played fairly. We Hungarians are said to be a nation of lawyers, and our top priority at present is to come up with a constitution: not until the government and the opposition have battled it out over every paragraph can we actually begin to play ball.

The feudal-like, tribal-like clans, the Communist old-boy network is likely to break down. The clever and the malleable are looking for a new kind of friend, a kind more or less forbidden until now. Superficially at least, the people who used to avoid meeting or even greeting dissidents are now a bit disconcerted and have resorted to gushing. The collapse of the hierarchy and chain of command has benefited those at the lower end of the power structure: they are simpler now and more realistic; they realize that latent public opinion cannot be kept latent forever. An entire society is trying to play born-again moralist. People make believe they are starting with a clean slate. No one did dirty deeds unless forced to from on high. As if fear were an excuse for immorality! The fact is, no one was free of the sin of compliance; merely by observing the rules of the game, you were an accomplice.

Much of what happens in this country today happens as a result of ill will, sarcasm, and an anxiety born of deep-seated pessimism. Yet no one could claim that life is more boring than it used to be. More Hungarians are reading newspapers, even though newspaper prices are up: there is a lot of interesting writing, and faces are more personal.

The standard of living is temporarily on the decline. Many people are spending their summer holidays at home, and every tenth Hungarian lives under the poverty line. The homeless are staking out benches with their bags, and the police have stopped hauling them off on the grounds of "criminal vagrancy."

The one-party system may have crumbled, but the authoritarian personality type—the one-party man, who will have no trouble learning the rightist slogans to replace his leftist ones—will be around for a long time. His type was not introduced to Hungarian history by the Communists; in fact, we would be hard put to pinpoint a period in Hungarian history as a legitimate place from which to start over.

People have been complaining there's too much politicking going on. As if there'd been none before! Keeping one's mouth shut was a form of politics. Not until this year did our society start calling things by their proper names, and like it or not, what comes into the open now will not soon be forgotten. Fear is hard to get over: only a minority has spoken out; the majority

is still silent. Under Communism everything was politics, everything human acquired a political slant; in this experimental
post-communist period we must formulate rules for the re-
trenchment of politics, for society's self-defense. Many Hungarians think freedom good even if it does not come with a full
shopping cart. Having seen that what we once thought impossible is in fact possible, we are deterined to win our end-of-
the-millennium match. We can no longer imagine the power
of speech being prized away from us.

I do not feel close to people who dine out on the revolution
of 1956, glorifying what was a university and street-corner event
in a rhetoric bordering on the official. Time has blown our frail
stories out of proportion.

Political freethinking and moral freethinking are growing
less and less compatible. A new group of highly serious, righ-
teously indignant people has come to the fore. Anyone who
says what was official doctrine two or three years ago they call
a raving lunatic, which is less a sign of liberation than of the
fact that a new official doctrine is in the making. Years ago I
remember hearing perfectly sensible young men and women
chanting slogans in favor of the total homogenization of society
and the total nationalization of private property and the means
of production; they were every bit as gung ho, as militant and
uncompromising as their counterparts today. Of course there
was more than ideological madness involved. Careers previously
undreamed of opened before them in the wake of the Communist takeover. The poor young workers and peasants who
made it through Party leadership training during the late forties
soon graduated to the black chauffeur-driven cars of the *nomenklatura.* Communism recruited its power elite from among

the little people—the slighted and bypassed, the uneducated and unsure of themselves—and organized it along military lines: if the Party said jump into the well, you jumped. The Party was our reason, our honor, our conscience. Things changed with the passing of time: today's Party elite came not so much from below and outside as from within, from the parvenus' offspring.

The new men come from outside again. They bear the rhetoric of the thirties. Communist kitsch has given way to a Christian-nationalist kitsch abounding in references to the conception of the state according to Saint Stephen and the cult of the Holy Crown, that is, cognitive curiosities that would bewilder the French, the English, or the Dutch. Since political discourse cannot be personal, since it must be couched in terms acceptable to the silent majority, the best of all possible diction is the one worn to a sheen. All that matters is how it sounds; it has no need to make a point.

When communist discourse proved hopeless, it was placed in mothballs for the retirement club of a certain geriatric minority. Not only can today's ruling class remain in power without the Communist Party; those among them who were Party members only yesterday consider it a hindrance: their careers would be better served by a national democracy oriented towards the West but tolerated by the East; they feel we should get on with the re-Christianization and Westernization process as quickly as possible.

The Communist bureaucracy will dissolve in the new civil society, which is all to the good, as is the fact that the current order has not reached for guns. The turncoats have accepted the West lock, stock, and barrel. The prime criterion for anything is currently: How does it work in America? Give the satellite mentality a great power—*any* great power—and it will swear loyalty to it. The *sensible* satellite mentality will try to gauge how much it stands to gain by its loyalty and how much it will have to suffer for it.

Today a resourceful, realistic elite is openly changing sides. For centuries the Hungarian nation as a political entity was more or less, by and large, by fits and by starts loyal to German-speaking west-central Europe. When German-speaking west-central Europe went mad, Hungary went from loyal small-time partner to satellite. Now that Hungary is turning back to its more highly developed Austro-German friends, it is careful to show them deference; yet it is proud to be closer to them than are the neighboring Slavs. There is a constant conflict between sovereignty and servility in the Hungarian character. (By servility we mean the attitude expected of underlings by a liege, bailiff, petty officer, or any representative of the law.) There is a suspiciousness towards the surrounding Slav-Orthodox culture and a sense of superiority with respect to all non-Germans in the region. For a time the very concept of the Hungarian nation seemed not only compatible but even congruent with German Europe. Now that the German West is an integral part of the West as such, there is fortunately no need to choose between two Wests. There is no harm therefore in simply calling it Europe. Now even the servile, satellite types have changed from the Leninist train to the democratic train. *Autres trains, autres moeurs.*

Once there was a country that was constantly behind the times, shunted off to the side, prone to disaster. It spent much of its energy explaining away its failures and grew accustomed to watching others pass it by, to making do, to stagnant, provincial self-pity. Then, suddenly—lo and behold—everything is in fast motion. The much-longed-for avalanche calls for bold-faced adaptability. The words are new, the face is old. The face is new, the words—their style, at least, is old. Crystal is more beautiful than aspic, but more fragile, too.

1989

Being Hungarian in Europe

Being Hungarian in Europe means not being alone. It means that among a hundred Europeans of various national persuasions we can expect a few Hungarians as well. We must not talk only among ourselves; we must talk to others, tell people in their own language what is of interest to them. People are appreciated in society for being congenial. If you are proud, hurt, jealous, and spiteful, you will have no friends—and another excuse to take offense. We all nurture within us the picture of a decent person, the kind we might want as, say, a neighbor. There is no reason why decorum and morality among individuals should differ from decorum and morality among nations.

Being European in Hungary means learning biblical democracy, in other words, that we are equals in every situation: at work, at table, in bed. The stronger—more densely populated and more productive—Western half of Europe has developed a set of political morals based on liberal democracy. Only those countries can be considered European in which the freedom of the individual is inviolable, human dignity is the alpha and omega of all values, and no group is persecuted for being different. Intimidating or constraining or killing one's fellowman for belonging to this or that group has become inimical to Europeans despite their long history of racial, national, and class hatred or, rather, because they have learned from their history and finally realize that discrimination leads to murder. Lording it over one's inferiors and cringing to one's superiors may have been acceptable to Europe's autocratic regimes, but such behavior, though still common, is considered an unfortunate remnant of backwardness by the citizens of Europe's free nations and is acceptable no longer. In the new Europe the only place for the tyrant/sycophant is the wax museum. Is democracy possible without democratic individuals? Democracy needs team players, not warriors.

For an American, Made in Europe means quality. When I look at our shop windows, at the state of our villages and towns, when I look at everything around me, I see how far below European standards we have sunk. Yesterday I watched while a Dutchman in a Budapest café waited twenty minutes for his coffee. The answer he got when he protested that the waitresses were all standing around talking to one another was, "You're in Budapest." In other words, sloppy work is the norm. For most Europeans we are what they can purchase and enjoy of our goods and services. Hence we are also Budapest, one of Europe's most beautiful and most polluted cities. We are not wax figures; we have fashioned ourselves and our city, made ourselves and our city what they are today. Freedom, like oppression, is work, the common creation of government and populace.

It is axiomatic that the entire populace is responsible—all

but entirely responsible—for its history, ideals, and traditions, the bad as well as the good: the shame is ours with the glory; we can't skim off like cream what happens to appeal to us. But European humanism in its various national forms—starting with biblical and classical reflections on political morality—provides a touchstone for good and evil, and before I go any further let me say that I see the body of European literature with all its writers and thinkers as a body of law. We all sense what is involved here even if we cannot quite pin it down. Recently we have also been vouchsafed a collection of statute law applicable to all humankind and encompassing the basic human and civil rights, which is meant to be supplemented by specific codicils on the part of individual European states.

Respect for human rights has its own logic. It leads to democracy. The western half of Europe has recognized the connection between the two as it has the connection between a freely thinking *Homo sapiens,* a freely acting *Homo economicus,* and a freely mediating *Homo politicus.* Any social experiment that obscures, challenges, or violates even one of these basic freedoms will be forced to turn against the others because both democratic and autocratic paradigms have a strict inner logic to them. Once you take the first step on the road to democracy, you will eventually take the next, and the next, and so on down the line. Once you start to reform an autocratic regime, you will eventually arrive at democracy.

The only way a nation can assure itself of equilibrium and continuity, the productive passage from one generation to the next, is by making the cultural, economic, and political freedoms of the individual the basic law of the land. Present-day Europe deems a nation worthy of respect only insofar as its state respects the people who constitute it, each and every one of them, and only insofar as its politicians derive its common values—each in his own way, of course—from values that are wholly compatible with the freedoms of the individual. There is no legal alternative to the respect for and logic of the basic human and civil rights. Every instance of freedom curtailed, every instance of discrimination is in violation of the political morality that is accepted throughout Europe and granted legal status by the European Parliament. The simple-minded cynicism that uses national, class, or any other interests to reduce the defense of human dignity to a matter of contingency has resulted in blinkered minds, mass stupefaction, autocratic regimes, and countless violent deaths. Both pseudo-historical nationalism and pseudo-scientific materialism have given rise to wars and camps. The ideal of national sovereignty does not justify a nation-state's infringing on the rights of the individuals or minorities living in it.

Europe's political morality authorizes anyone to intervene in the internal affairs of a country, neighboring or distant, and stand up against the violation of human rights. Such is the principle on which Amnesty International bases its operations. It is a principle that has been on the rise since the seventies (witness the tendency first in Southern Europe, then in Latin America and Southeast Asia for military or one-party dictatorships to give way to civil democracies), and without it the political avalanche in Eastern Europe could not have taken place. Modern East European humanism, which came out of the dissident democratic movements and matured by battling the strut, spasms, and hysteria of collective egos, has taken deep root in our culture, and without it Hungary 1989 could not have taken place. I might add that this year's peaceful revolutions—our own and the analogous ones in a number of

Central and East European countries—have opened a new chapter in the history of European autonomy.

Every nation, every ethnic entity, every community, every group of people, every class in school, and even every family has its own unmistakable, complex character, a character more aesthetically discernible than scientifically definable. Its own individuality. If generalizations about an individual are lame, how much lamer are generalizations about a group of individuals. It takes artistic empathy to understand a community. People who brand communities with preconceived notions have cold, abstract, noninquisitive minds and make no attempt to understand even the people closest to them. The only way to raise national identity to respectability is to plumb its innate connection with personal identity, and the ground on which the personal and national meet is art. I do not mean to narrow the issue. I merely wish to offer the following hypothesis: assuming that our industrial society manages to avoid ecological catastrophe, it will be forced to grow into an artistic society.

Although most of the world media have given us top marks for our performance this year, recent visitors have observed an odd, even grotesque phenomenon: while the economy falters, the main concern of certain democratic forces is how to beat down other democratic forces. The combination of hatred and political rivalry is most repugnant. A nation is its style, after all; we are, as I have said, what we make ourselves. Besides, the media are listening in, telling the world what we say—the ugly things too—and people are losing sympathy for us. No one enjoys mud-slinging—the recriminations, the fireworks, the cheap pronunciamentos that go along with freer speech. Ignorance, poverty, and oppression do not help. Democratic revolutions of oppressed and self-oppressing societies bring all manner of unsavory matters to light. The kind of country we must create now is one Europeans will appreciate even after they come to know it. Neither self-praise nor self-flagellation is characteristic of a growing nation. Our record for this year is quite decent. Let's not make a mess of it after our first free New Year's Eve.

1989

A New Year's Prediction for 1990

The spirit of the democratic revolution has made great strides in East-Central Europe. Every one-party paternalistic system carries the seeds of a democratic revolution. In the past few weeks panic-stricken parliaments packed with Communist representatives have been busy dethroning the ruling Communist parties. The idea of a multiparty, constitutional, parliamentary democracy has triumphed. The state whose legitimacy derives from one party is on its way out, and bursting in with youthful ardor to take its place is the spirit of the *Rechtsstaat,* the state whose legitimacy derives from the rule of law.

The dramatic avalanche was preceded by a long period of erosion. A piece of cloth tears suddenly after years of invisible wear. The idea of "superiority in uniformity" is worn to threads and no longer tenable. Why should everyone be the same? What's wrong with variety?

Southern Europe's fascistoid dictatorships fell apart during the sixties; Eastern Europe's communist dictatorships fell apart in 1989. An edifying coincidence, one might say: an homage, at a remove of two hundred years, to the revolution that first proclaimed the civil rights of the individual.

Inviolable dominions have been brought low; feudal absolutisms have turned into civil states; democracy has encircled the northern hemisphere. The Soviet area will come up with nothing better: recent experience shows democracy to be the sole form of government that provides the equilibrium and stability necessary to keep each change in leadership from becoming a change in regime.

It is a fact that democracies do not wage war with one another and do their best to minimize internal violence; it is a fact that liberal democracy is compatible not only with the world market but also with reform and self-regulation, while the logic of the one-party system opposes reform, that is, leads to its own eventual demise.

This year people living all over Central Europe came to the realization that communism is less satisfactory a form of government than democracy; what is more, they felt strong enough to act on it: they have intimate knowledge of dictatorships of the right and left and were fed up with both varieties, and suddenly the influence of the dissident movements reached the critical mass that sent them into the streets to take over their own public space.

The democratic epidemic shows how closely related we are: we stimulate one another, infect one another. The chain reaction is one more proof that Central Europe exists.

Even the Soviet Union has the makings of a democratic revolution. Yes, if our time has a world-historical process, it is the spread of the logic of democracy, and the intelligentsia has served as matchmaker between Hegel's world-soul and liberal democracy.

The West has proved stronger than the East. If there is no war, the West is stronger, the West being a civil society, the East—a feudal one.

The formation of a middle class (*embourgeoisement, Verbürgerlichung*) is on its way again. A process artificially cut short now resumes its forward march. The past cannot be buried. But neither can the pupil skip a year: there is no world-view master key to open the door of knowledge.

Pluralism is taking shape over all Central Europe and the Soviet Union. Not even the rhetoric of democratic socialist reform seems likely to prolong the life of one-party state socialism. Communism may be able to survive only in its most classical form, that is, in Albania, Romania, or North Korea, where cracks in the wall of autocracy are quickly caulked and the devil of laxity and liberalization is denied so much as a foothold.

The orthodox communists of East-Central Europe lack the power to stage a neo-Stalinist counterrevolution and the blood feud it would most likely entail. In decadent and demoralizing times like these even secret police chiefs may find themselves behind bars; under certain conditions you have to pass up the idea of a coup no matter how much it appeals to you. The Bolshevik ideological furor that justified beating-imprisonment-execution has come to an end, and when radical youth east of the Iron-Curtain-turned-relic thinks of radical deeds, the last thing it has in mind is a communist utopia.

What it thinks of is Europe. Europe and its history as accumulated capital. Even from here on the Danube it is plain to see that Europe is moving in the direction of large-scale integration on the one hand and small-scale independent regionalism on the other. The utopia of democratic federalism is real. For the first time in history Europe has begun to take shape as an economic unit, one that puts mutual trade above national expansion. Earlier French and German—and the more recent American and Russian—plans for hegemony have failed. The concept of "major power" has lost its meaning in Europe.

National independence movements, coupled for the most part with democratic movements, are catching on throughout Eastern Europe. There is democratic nationalism and there is authoritarian nationalism; there is pluralistic nationalism and there is fundamentalist nationalism.

A new philosophy of power is making itself felt, a power that eschews violence. After the Second World War the Europe that ended where the Soviet bloc began was pushed into the background as a military power—and only then came into its own. What mattered, Europeans realized, was the kind of lives they lived, not the childish issue of who could kill whom. They could hardly threaten, anyway, their arsenals being little more than closely watched scrap heaps.

The road to peace leads through freedom. There is no place without freedom. Dictatorships make unreliable partners for democracies because they make unreliable partners for their own citizens. Failure to recognize this fact vitiated the peace rhetoric from the start. Divided though Europe still is, let us hope that as the century comes to a close it will not spark off yet another world war.

Networks large and small are crisscrossing the continent, paying less and less attention to political and administrative borders. Federalism and regionalism walk arm in arm. The centralist reign of the capital city has drawn to a close, and towns of all shapes and sizes are welcome to join the European Urban Individualists Club. A new age is dawning, an artistic age, in which the value of both cities and works of art will come from the rich imagination inherent in their relationship. The new Europe is alive with activity, because every part of it longs to strike out on its own and try something new. We belong to an age whose workforce is pliable, flexible, eager to learn.

The preservation and renewal of traditions and institutions is the order of the day. Now that we're back on the train, let's not let things rush past us, let's be observant tourists. But there's a good deal coming into our homes as well: books, pictures, people. The computer has diminished the realm of personal communication. Rendering our microenvironments more livable is increasingly important, and that is poles apart from endless trade and consumption. We need internal architecture more than housing complexes. Being first is not what counts; it's doing the job right. We millenarians must pay greater respect to what is personal and intimate, to pottering, to leisure.

Revolution always comes as a surprise, especially to the instigators. I had occasion to talk to a fine Czech dissident writer two months ago. Oh no, he said, not in Czechoslovakia: the standard of living was higher and more stable than in Hungary; the workers were not particularly dissatisfied, the students not particularly active, and the party was so united! In time, maybe, in a few years . . . And what did we see on television but hundreds of thousands of people overrunning the squares of Prague and Bratislava and standing up to rubber truncheons. Where did these crowds come from? Out of the melancholy the Czechs like to call their own? In any case, it was a Prague and a Bratislava with human faces emerging from hiding, from the long hibernation of uniformity, and all those faces flashing past the cameras looked so interesting, so much like their Hungarian counterparts: young East-Central Europeans suddenly ecstatic about the taste of freedom. The fact that they even thought freedom possible took the wind out of the Politburo's sails; it proved that revolution is a game of symbols and gestures in which armed intimidators succeed only if people let themselves be intimidated, and if for some unknown reason they do not, then the intimidators themselves feel intimidated and their weapons turn into so much scrap metal. The startling shift in power may also be explained by the fact that people who lie don't exist while people who don't lie do. Who is which is bound to come out eventually.

Our neighbors to the north—Czechs and Slovaks and the Hungarian minority in Slovakia—have once more given flesh to the autonomy of the spirit in the heart of Europe; they have come together with their neighbors—Poles, East Germans, Hungarians—to form one interconnected region, one stage for the Central European revolution. We were very wrong not to coordinate our efforts to bring about freedom during the past hundred and fifty years, we who have known and suffered the same oppression and face the same formidable problems.

How can we make democracy out of communism in our own backyard? How can we conjure up or back a middle class, without which no economy can function? How can we establish civilized communication among every interested individual in our population? Only now will we begin to see the face, the figure, the true essence of the geographical concept of Central Europe. When most of what we saw of one another was our

Party leaders, there was little love lost among us. What makes a country interesting is the interesting things its inhabitants are up to. Now our four countries are busy dismantling autocratic, absolutist regimes, something we all had experience with in the nineteenth century as well (communism being only a more modern and effective variant of its predecessors).

One of our jobs is to extend the "dismantling" metaphor to ourselves: we must slough off our psyches, rethink our values, reorganize our personalities, inspect every aspect of our biographies. Which is not always an elevating experience. There are those who divert attention from the shouts raised against them by outshouting them, and those who now raise their fists in situations where only yesterday they clapped their hands.

I am certain that the political philosophies of East-Central Europeans will exert a powerful influence on one another, and I am glad of it for selfish reasons: I hope the public exchange of views among our region's democrats will have a sobering, civilizing, even mildly mocking effect on us.

Many people have been asking themselves: How could it have taken decades for us to say and do things that seem so self-evident today? What sort of crippling spell lay on us? If things were one way then and another now, can we now trust our then selves?

In the present situation artists and scholars can be both participants in and observers of the mythological phenomenon that we call history and that on some days seems miraculous only because it was impossible the day before. Artists and scholars have set the stage for these changes by setting forth believable human truths in their work. In a culture of lies truthful statements act like antibodies: they nourish moral fortitude in others, strangers, who suddenly condense into a decisive social force. When the history of the 1989 East European political landslide is written, the spread of the influence of word and image will be a particularly exciting topic.

Nineteen eighty-nine was the year of liberation in East-Central Europe, the year many people lost the habit of fear and acquired the habit of freedom of expression. I sincerely hope we have taken history's lesson seriously and will never again give up our right to freedom, even if yesterday's freedom fighters suggest that it is only temporary and in the interest of some higher goal.

By abolishing the one-party system, we have abolished feudal differences, privileges for individuals. Political equality and linguistic and cultural equality are inseparable. We don't want people's human dignity to be insulted merely because their mothers spoke the language of a national minority. We don't want our borders to impede our movement; we reject the isolationist nationalism of dictatorships. This is a time for us to learn from one another. Accustomed though we are to looking east and west, let us increasingly look north and south. The fact is that ever since Czechoslovakia, East Germany, and Bulgaria joined the nonviolent democratic revolution, we ourselves have moved farther west.

It is an extraordinary feeling to go to Bratislava and be invited by friends to speak freely to a crowd of a hundred and fifty thousand in the main square. Part of me was utopian enough to expect this kind of thing, but the realist in me called it a pipe dream. Reality has proved the realist wrong. The people who turned out to be right were those who assumed they were not alone in wanting human equality and dignity, which are incompatible with the truncheon as trump card. A veritable *coup de théâtre:* the entire population of East-Central Europe changes its way of life and celebrates it by pouring out into the squares in sequences tailor-made for television.

1989

Thoughts on the Reconciliation of Christians and Jews

The Bible is a book of multiple authorship, the book of a people that has created its own God. Powerful individuals beckon us, the audience, as they spread the Word, transfigured, among the nations. But when they are alone and continue their dialogue with the one and only God, none of them is completely at one with Him: some have this to say, others that. And, like all authors, they are all fallible. We read them for what they have to tell us about exceptional personalities and experiences.

Both Jewish and Christian fundamentalists consider religion a sacrosanct tradition; indeed, they are in such agreement that they consider any true dialogue impossible. In this they resemble Muslim and, yes, communist fundamentalists. If Jews and Christians do not wish to see themselves as fundamentalists, they must search their rich tradition for its pluralist strains. Otherwise no significant dialogue is in fact possible. If Judaism and Christianity wish to survive, they must reexamine everything that has occurred during the two thousand years since biblical

times; they must also take a third spiritual authority into account, namely, world literature (in the broadest sense of the
term), for which a centralist hierarchy is unthinkable.

Jewish pluralism existed in biblical times, in Talmudic
times, and in rabbinical times, and if we read Jewish writers of
the past two centuries we find that it exists today as well.
Christian pluralism has not had an easy time of it, but ever
since the Enlightenment the Christian religions have come to
a relatively tolerant modus vivendi. Then, too, the most important strain of political Christianity, the Christian democrats,
regards pluralism as integral to its self-image.

When the elder and younger siblings stand hand in hand
gazing over the planet, they see more and more people professing
different beliefs (whether they believe in them or not). Only
one fourth of the world population has roots in the Judeo-
Christian tradition. The time has come for a multilateral, global
discourse on religion. But conversation does not necessarily
mean conversion. We shall all remain as we were; we shall
merely understand one another better.

The relationship between an individual and God will continue to be a drama. Individuals tend to seek a support beyond
themselves and believe, when times are good, that they have
found it, but times change and the separation of God and
existence may no longer seem necessary.

Jews do not magnify the God-become-man or man-become-
God; they are aware that the teachers of the faith claim to have
heard God's word and they are willing to hear them out, but
what they place above all else is ceremony, which sanctifies
family life.

There are people for whom God is an integral part of existence, and because He is in ·everything, they do not wish to

speak of Him separately. Do they speak to Him or to their
conscience? They beg Him to stand by them, and when He
fails—"Why hast Thou abandoned me?"—they rue it bitterly.
The relationship between the individual and God, which our
mortality makes so dramatic, is a private, highly personal matter. It has little to do with those who make a profession of
professing His name.

Now that socialist state culture has collapsed, people are
looking for a simplified substitute, a simple opposite. Those
among them who have only recently discovered the Christian
in them may develop a taste for anti-Semitic remarks. Prestige
having lately moved from state to church, the insecure may
well seek security in religious terminology. From chapel to
Party, from Party to chapel. I am therefore suspicious of people
who switch pell-mell from socialist jargon to theological jargon.
They are merely replacing one form of intolerance with another.
Theirs is a prestige-based, one-book, fundamentalist mentality,
the kind that bludgeons its rivals with pious doctrine. Only
yesterday Tartuffe was a Marxist-Leninist. What is he today?

Clear-thinking Jews and Christians do not regard the recent
changes in terms of salvation. We have not been freed from
natural disasters or human evil. In other words, every good deed
still represents a grain of salvation. Salvation? Absolution. Ap-
peasement. Reconciliation. Repose. Sleep everlasting. Release
from the agonies of human existence. "His death came as a
blessing."

To maintain the practice of burning people alive we need
institutions that take no spiritual issue with murder and conceal
their true feelings in gibberish. There will always be friction
and jealousy among younger and older siblings. Reconciliation
presupposes mutual investigation. But from what angle? Not

from opposing spiritual trenches. No, we live in the here and now: we are more than Christians or Jews; we are fairly secularized Christian and Jewish Hungarians, Europeans, not particularly devout in the aggregate, and we can come up with nothing better than political equality and moral and metaphysical impartiality. Yet what reconciles Christians and Jews to one another—and to the rest of humanity, in some measure at least—is the idea of basic human rights.

It takes a good deal more to describe a person than to say he is a Jew or she a Christian. We must be careful to avoid pompous abstraction, the newly possible turn from left-think to right-think, from required atheism to required piety: both infringe on freedom of conscience. Religion and politics do not make good bedfellows. If we fail to keep them separate, we shall confuse two essentially different dimensions of human activity and lose the ability to speak precisely about either.

Dialogue derigidifies. The challenge to participants on both sides is to revitalize their religion, create personal variations on its spirit. People must not surrender freedom of conscience to any human institution, state-run or church-run; by failing to stand up for their convictions, they open the way for autocrats and tyrants. In the face of this inauspicious possibility, however, the European experience has shown human dignity to be indestructible.

1990

Revolution or Reform
(with Iván Szelényi)

Twentieth-century Hungarian history has been defined by right-ist and leftist revolutionary experiments that promise—after the defeat of an internal enemy or the formation of radically new structures and elites—to replace the old, rotting society with a new, healthy, cohesive one, a society free of conflict. The rightists promised racial, that is, ethnic homogeneity, the leftists homogeneity on the basis of class origin. The experiments of both proved unsuccessful except in causing untold suffering.

Most thinking Hungarians hope that the country's latter-day political democracy will revive the often interrupted development of a Hungarian middle class. We are inclined to regard the current transition in Hungary as reform rather than revolution or counterrevolution, though we cannot rule out the danger of its leading to the creation of new order with a new revolutionary rhetoric.

Generalizing from the history of philosophy and from social ethics, we hold that reform movements are in the long run more effective and more humane than revolutions. They humiliate fewer people, are less damaging to self-respect, disrupt fewer lives and families, and are less likely to punish the innocent. Concepts like "calling to account," "settling scores," and "retaliation" are part and parcel of the concept of revolution, and the demands of "revolutionary justice" push civil law into the background.

Revolutionary dynamics fosters the belief that there is one overriding truth and that it can be represented solely by the ideologically pure—a belief that legitimizes the ever increasing power of the vanguard (that is, the Party), the sole source of ideologically pure thinkers. Consequently, what the ideology labels "correct" its followers must consider positive and its enemies negative. The bourgeois mind is skeptical of such an approach: it posits a variety of truths and interests and is therefore tolerant of, and even curious about, ideas differing from its own basic way of thinking.

Another reason we hope the present turn to a bourgeois society will be more a matter of reform than revolution is that it will mean less of a wrench in people's lives. We now know how unjust the wholesale condemnation of the interwar elite, urban middle class, peasantry, and civil servants proved to be; we know that the collective discrimination it caused forced large numbers of people to feel shame for their past and even hide it.

Yet now as ever it is clear that the purity and moral legitimacy of those who make the most noise about injustice need to be questioned. The ideological fervor of the neophyte, the hope on the part of the mediocre that politics will let them run rings around the talented, the compulsion of yesterday's collaborators to point the finger at others in an effort to divert attention from themselves—such less-than-noble motives, grudges in search of targets, and plain old envy go hand in glove with the revolutionary's call for revenge. Let us hope that as the twentieth century draws to a close, the newly revitalized Hungarian middle class will find a way to temper these inhumane East European propensities.

All Hungarians now middle-aged or older have spent the major part of their lives under state socialism and have no desire to think of virtually their entire adult past as a dark age of shame and defeat. Critical self-examination is by no means alien to their mentality, but they would like to see a certain continuity in their lives and the lives of their families, a modicum of respect for themselves and their principles. The life experience of a generation or two cannot be simply written off. Just as it made no sense to reduce a thousand years of Hungarian history to the bleak tableau of "enslavement and servility," it would be mindless to condemn all that happened over the past few decades and all the players in a drama in which after all each of us had a role.

If we had to sum up the essence of a civil society in one sentence, we would refer to what might be called the autonomy of the spheres, that is, the fact that in a civil society politics is separate from administration, the economy, science, culture, and religion. Who belongs or belonged to which political party or who professes or professed which political principles is a private affair.

If we truly wish to change our system, we cannot be satisfied with one party's taking the other's place. That would be no

more than a change in government. Changing the system entails changing the very rules of the game. In a civil society the
only people eligible for nonpolitical positions are those who are
professionally qualified and have proved their worth.

Political discrimination has decimated the reserve of Hungarian professionals on more than one occasion in the course
of this century. It began with the revolutionary Hungarian
Communist regime in 1919 and the counterrevolutionary regime that toppled it, continued with the persecution of the
Jews during the thirties and forties, and resumed after 1945,
when the Communists first declared all bourgeois professionals
their enemies, systematically removing them from positions
of power, and later turned on their own, less-than-reliable,
Communist-trained professionals as well. Finally, there were
the waves of emigration of professionals following each political
upheaval. The greater the political disaster, the greater the
pressure on them to leave. Convinced as we are that a new
wave of political discrimination would once more set back the
development of a Hungarian middle class, we hope that professionally qualified civil servants, managers, journalists, and sci-
entists will remain in positions commensurate with their
abilities.

It is only natural that in a multiparty democracy people
elected to office should change when the party in power
changes. But public administration, if it is to be professional,
requires that musical chairs be limited to the highest echelons.
The day-to-day functions on both the national and local levels
must be carried out by professional civil servants, for whom
they represent a lifelong career. This dual arrangement ensures
that policies will be revitalized yet continuity maintained.

During our earlier research we met a number of heads of

agricultural cooperatives and officials of ministries and local councils and the like who, given the framework within which they had to operate, did a perfectly decent, honest job. We might add that in the late seventies the Kádár regime started reversing state socialism's virtually official policy of counter-selection by appointing qualified professionals to state and even Party functions. The very fact that this new elite began to behave like a professional intelligentsia was a major factor in the relatively civilized, nonviolent transition from communism to the current regime. It would be both senseless and unfair to brand these key transition figures as collaborators and exclude them from participation in future regimes. We would especially stress the virtue of this ethical and social stance in the politically neutral realm of science and culture—politically neutral in the sense that its practitioners weigh pros and cons rather than carry out political goals.

If research and teaching posts on the university and academy levels, positions of leadership in the institutes of art and literature, and prizes for outstanding achievement in the arts and sciences continue to be allotted on the basis of political loyalty—now divided among the followers of several parties instead of one—then we will have yet another revival of our East European feudal tradition. Proponents of grafting this one-party principle onto a multiparty system may try to defend it by claiming it is only a temporary measure necessary to rectify former injustices, but we feel that once instated it would be likely to gain a foothold.

We are at a crossroads. We can go the route of revolutionary rhetoric, which promises quick results but in fact, in our experience, holds a nation back. Or we can choose the political approaches we deem to be the most evenhanded, the ones likely to harm as few people as possible. We are convinced that this humanitarian strategy is not only more virtuous than the cult of revolution; we are convinced that it is more effective as well.

1990

The Melancholy of Rebirth

Switching to a new system of government is inevitably disenchanting, perhaps because of the eschatological expectations it is bound to raise. A hopeful mood takes hold: everything will improve once a parliamentary government has replaced single-party rule. People want to believe they will feel at home in their own country.

When you live under a dictatorship, you imagine that with a change in regime even the leaves will turn green. If the country is a closed camp and the Iron Curtain has no cracks, your room is a cell. Once the Iron Curtain crumbles, you look at your room and say, "Time for a little remodeling."

What kind? Radical reform? Quiet revolution? Shock therapy? "Oh dear," you think, tired of inertia yet afraid of insecurity. "Are we in for hard times? Will the new system repair our houses and increase our pensions? Will yesterday's bastard be today's hero? Will my joints stop killing me?"

Where is the turn for the better to come from? From us.

From the fact that we ourselves have made a turn for the better. Great expectations cause great disappointments, but perhaps the expectations themselves are of the essence. Our country has always been what *we* are and will presumably continue to be so: state and people are a fairly accurate reflection of each other.

On the whole I feel better about the general state of things than before, when the System with a capital S held sway. Interesting—the System is no more. It was; it's gone. I used to criticize the System; now I criticize individual things and do my best not to reconstitute a system out of them.

I have less to fear. I have evolved from phantom to citizen. I have a place. Of course if you'd asked me in 1986 how I felt, I'd have said, "Fine, thank you." True, I'd just had a son. But even if you'd asked me in, say, 1987, I'd have given the same answer. (Though in that year I had another son.)

Nineteen eighty-eight was a good year, because it brought an end to the conservative monarchy of the Moscow-anointed and locally tolerated János Kádár. But even though we began to fidget a bit, we were still perfectly comfortable with the kingdom's stability and *Gemütlichkeit.* Everyone had a way of getting by. It was the period of "No news, thank God."

What the change means to me? My censorship troubles are over: people can read what I write without the allusions imposed by secrecy and prohibition. I have a forum for what I wish to say—as has anyone with the slightest aptitude for writing, and of course anyone with no aptitude whatever. I no longer need apply for exit and entrance visas, and the border guards of more and more countries simply wave me through when I show my passport. I am no longer searched when I leave the country, so

I can pack my manuscripts along with my socks. The *ancien régime* had its delights, but the body search was not among them.

I was not alone in experiencing the odd relief that came from crossing over to the West: no more barbed wire, no more watch towers—they couldn't catch us anymore, couldn't take away our passports, which after all belonged to them, not us. The whole point of the System was to make us feel that we were in their hands, that they could do with us as they pleased, that anything was possible. The personnel of a dictatorship can afford to indulge its whims. It cripples, even paralyzes the population by making punishment an everpresent threat. That is its purpose. Loyal trepidation—such was the collective magnum opus of our state and our people. Now it, too, will be a thing of the past.

The country has not totally fallen apart; it is in fact more colorful, energetic, resourceful than before. It has a bit of everything: sophistication, vulgarity—this is a Balzacian age. Budapest today bears some resemblance to Budapest at the turn of the century, that is, the bourgeoisie is making a comeback. Purity and variety are far from synonyms.

I enjoy coming home from neighboring countries. There's always the chance I'll find a late-night restaurant near the border, a place where I can get a decent meal and cordial smile. Everything is in good supply, there are no lines, I have no great trouble locating what I need, services function normally.

Prices are up, poverty is on the rise, the homeless population is increasing, but the people in the street are for the most part tastefully or at least tolerably dressed. The harsh, indigent, East-European side of the city will be with us for a long time to come, but even now the Budapest street scene does not differ dramatically from, say, its Viennese counterpart.

Resignation and neglect, depression and regression belong to yesterday. Many of my friends are involved in new projects. I see active, dedicated people everywhere. Gone is the once ubiquitous plaint about how meaningless work is. I detect a mild decrease in stress, an occasional wry smile. Work is possible.

People talk to me in the street, nod, exchange pleasantries. It's a new experience. I have readers to write for. I can see them.

From capitalism via fascism and communism back to capitalism. In other words, capitalist development was interrupted by a pointless intermezzo, a violent, hysterical assault lasting from 1914 to 1989 and called the twentieth century. The less said about it the better.

By now, oddly enough, I all but take for granted the new tranquillity, that is, the fact that the probability of an East-West war in Europe, in our cities, is practically nil and tanks are moving out on trains. But it is due in large part to the bloc-eroding work done by autonomous movements here in Eastern Europe. In other words, we took an active part in the process.

We have left the gate of an imaginary extermination camp, pinching ourselves in disbelief. The possibility that we will die a natural death is growing steadily, though death is never natural. The kind of life we live—peaceful, sad—will now be our own doing. Less danger, more responsibility.

The American and Russian elites are condemned to co-operation, and that is good for Europe or, rather, for those regions that have cooled down and put their national, religious,

and ideological hysterias behind them. Eventually the sole jus-
tifiable use of arms will be that sanctioned by the UN Security
Council: operations by a world police force against mafias that
violate international law or dictators who become intolerable.
Not too close to home, I hope (if I may be both selfish and
cautious).

Turning our backs on world war, imperialism, and dictatorship, we saw the end of history, we saw a golden age of
capitalist democracy; we dreamed of the end of dissident culture,
we dreamed of a new, autonomous culture. And then the Per-
sian Gulf flared up. Perhaps the twentieth century isn't over
after all, or are we merely moving into the twenty-first?

Nineteen eighty-nine was the year of Eastern Europe, the year
of breakthrough, of choice, of saying what had to be said. Now
we are no longer front-page news. The fact that there is less
and less "communist" about us is less and less sensational. The
wave of change has broken over us and moved on, farther east;
we hear more authoritarian states come crashing down. The
cameras have moved on too, and tourists and businessmen are
taking their place. Now, after East-Central Europe, the Balkans
and the former Soviet Union are in the spotlight; now Eastern
Europe proper is the scene of the most dramatic changes, the
hotbed of a new national consciousness. For years the empire
kept nationalist sentiment under control; now every repressed
bit of it is coming to the surface.

We want a civil society, which means we still lack full-fledged
civil rights. If we still resist identifying with capital property,
it is because we have none. Yet clearly capitalism is the price
we must pay for democracy, and we accept it—some gleefully,

others with a certain reserve. Considering how "scientific" socialism was, I will not be surprised if our capitalism turns out to be more theory- than profit-oriented; after all, state-trained intellectuals have more to say about the transition to capitalism than do independent entrepreneurs.

Everything that smacks of socialism gets low marks nowadays. Yesterday's Communists are denounced as the prime culprits for today's ills. People who until recently held out for reform within the planned economy have suddenly turned monetarist, that is, intransigent enemies of the very idea of socialism. As far as the poor are concerned, however, nothing has changed: they are still ignored.

Have socialist values lost all their worth? Is it valid to demand that everyone, even a do-nothing, should have the right to eat, that even the poor should have the right to education or heath care? Western socialism is really nothing but a legally mandated corrective to capitalism, a safety net offered by the community to the individual in case of extreme need. Western socialism exists even if it goes by different names, but it calls for wide-ranging self-government, not the aggressive expansion of centralized power. Its highest values have nothing to do with the state; they aim at safeguarding the existence of the individual, even an individual unable to keep up with the competition. It holds that every person, every household, every community is an entity unto itself, that the idea of a collective working in solidarity to help the individual and protect the individual's freedom is in no way opposed to the development of a capitalist class (the *embourgeoisement* of society), that it is in fact the highest stage of capitalist development.

Today's radicals have a hard time imagining that yesterday's radicals were no less willing to make sacrifices and no less well-intentioned than themselves. Admittedly, the language was different. Yesterday's radicals wished to overcome the egoism of the individual and, spurning their parents' collaboration and servility, placed duty above freedom. People who use the new language feel superior to people still attached to the old language and therefore unable to adapt quickly and easily.

Hungary now stands between socialism and capitalism. We are a kind of composite of the two, an amalgam. Even though I hear daily that socialism is dead, I find it very much alive, at least the variety that until recently was called "real" or "existing" socialism. What lives on is the instinctive attempt on the part of the central government to secure all positions of power and impose a common worldview that will foster cultural and political homogeneity.

Capitalism in Hungary today is more hope than reality. When people spoke about socialism with enthusiasm, they were only dimly aware of what it entailed. Soon they were up to their necks in *state* socialism. That was easy. Now they are trying to climb out of it. That is hard indeed. And although they appear to be making a hook-or-crook kind of progress, people who have served the state with equanimity are not particularly eager to work for private entrepreneurs: they do not relish the thought of being at a boss's mercy. Not that the bosses at state enterprises were a pleasure to work for, but people who stayed on there were bound to outlast several bosses and thus felt that the enterprise belonged more to them than to the succession of short-lived overseers. There is such a thing as having an emotional stake in an enterprise, being a part of the machinery, so to speak.

As long as socialism was strong, the welfare state assured

the shrewd and/or faithful a comfortable existence. Now that such assurance has fallen by the wayside, absenteeism is going out of style. We used to live by our wits; now there are fewer opportunities for slipping away from work to go shopping, keep a tryst, do a bit of moonlighting. Not even the radical anti-socialists had ever experienced a capitalist boss. Some people were more courageous, some more cautious, but as long as you differed from the POWERS THAT BE, as long as you gave THEM trouble, you were all right. THEY, on the other hand, stuck their noses in everybody's business and made trouble. A lot of time and energy was wasted on this not particularly clever parlor game.

An era is coming to an end, an era of keeping to oneself (which was as much a part of the royal existence of state so-cialism as the dissident movement), an era of drinking, cursing, shrugging one's shoulders and saying, "What's the point? It won't get you anywhere. Keep your nose clean." Now many people feel challenged to show what they can do.

We have less time for one another. We used to shut our-selves up in our apartments and discuss the things we couldn't read in the papers, our "antiworld," as if were. As the visible world loses its ambiguities, we are growing as boring as we in fact are.

I was twelve in 1945, when fascism was overthrown in Hungary. Until then we were under the Horthy regime, which had re-mained in power throughout the Arrow Cross years. Until 1945 my position as a Jew was rather vulnerable. Had the Horthy regime held out a few weeks more, I would not be sitting here making these observations.

I was fifteen in 1948, when Communism took over in

Hungary, and not until 1990, by which time I was fifty-seven, did parliamentary elections bring the monopoly of the Party to an end. After the victory of Communism my position as a young bourgeois (that is, someone whose name was ticked off on every list as a class enemy) was vulnerable again.

From the point of view of both regimes I was born tainted. I thus experienced their disapproval not as a person but as a creature belonging to first a racial category, then a social category doomed to extinction. What I was actually like never entered the picture: I was guilty by definition. I of course rebelled and was immediately—and rightly—classified as a dissident. And while there is nothing inherently hazardous about being born a Hungarian Jew, I cannot, as I gaze upon the current spiritual horizon of my homeland, rule out the possibility of a new vulnerability.

Communism, unlike fascism, never tried to murder me; it merely tried to make me its loyal subject. I never forget the difference. The most important things that can happen to a person happened to me between the ages of fifteen and seventeen, in the era of Communism. I am a *ci-devant*, a reactionary from those incredible, grotesque times.

Certain aspects of our new political life I find quite gratifying. There are a few politicians—in the president's chair, in Parliament, in the government—whose mind and style I quite admire. Then again, politics is growing less important: I am less dependent on it. In retrospect I wonder whether we didn't blow it out of proportion. All I want from a regime is that it keep its distance: I don't want it to ban me or uphold me, just to leave me alone. I want it to do its job courteously, like the staff of a fine hotel. I want it to minister to my needs, not threaten me. I pay the bill—in taxes—and expect the staff to earn its keep. Which is more or less what seems to be happening. The trouble is, hotels take time to mellow.

Hungarian politics has been centrist for more than the past two years; it has been centrist for the past two decades—toning issues down, avoiding confrontation, seeking a middle road, that is, pursuing a relatively predictable, conservative program of reform. This middle-of-the-road approach, which a sardonic observer might call weathercock politics or just plain opportunism, can therefore boast of a certain continuity. Our malicious observer will also detect a talent for knowing which way the wind blows in the shift from east to west: in this part of the world the more powerful overlord is always right. We like to say that our greatest virtue is the ability to survive, and we like to call it realism. Neither our tradition nor our geography promotes idealism or philosophical consistency.

There is something typically Hungarian about the conviction that a liberal reform must be carried out by a conservative government. For better or for worse the government must follow that logic. The new class of Hungarian politicians, with a few exceptions, appears to be possessed of self-control.

The political celebrities of the previous era are growing helpless before our eyes: they are being dragged through the mud and forced from their posts, occasionally even from their flats. I for one would not be happy to see a new contingent of overlords moving into those flats. I saw it once and it was not a pretty sight.

Envy is everywhere, the desire for revenge rampant. The people who have emerged in the wake of the changes have certain features in common. Not even they quite understand how it all came about, how they ended up on top, but as they settle into their new functions, they take it for granted that their ranks and titles were foreordained.

Yesterday's gung-ho Party members, now disillusioned and removed from their posts, have withdrawn from politics; yesterday's Party leaders are keeping a jaundiced eye on their successors, wondering how they will adapt, rehearsing the roles of marginalization and inner emigration made popular only yesterday—by today's new celebrities.

"For half a century I served an evil cause," says a sprightly old man.

What is the proper response?

"Next time choose your cause more carefully."

Everything long buried can now come out—but only if it was there to begin with. The normal, healthy man in the street is less turncoat than sponge: he soaks up whatever comes along and is utterly convinced that he has always believed what he now says.

Communist rhetoric has collapsed and pulled the social democrats down with it. The only game in town is between the neoconservatives and liberals. The pendulum has swung to the right, so this is not the time to ask what the left is up to; people are giving the left a wide berth. If you're prudent, you know that the place to be is on the moderate right. The clientele for radical-right rhetoric—for the time being, at least—is small.

Even as society represses the memory of its recent tendency to adapt, reliable Communists are turning into reliable national-

ists. A number of buzzwords have been enlisted in the process. Leaders have no trouble finding parties, and speeches
are easy to learn. The eternal leader points an accusatory
finger at a former colleague who failed to switch allegiance
in time. I hear praises sung to the weathercock mentality: consistency is a virtue of the simpleminded, says an intelligent man
I know; anyone incapable of change is senile. Morality cracks,
and the weathercock spins on. We've seen them before:
wheeler-dealers making their way to the top, life imitating art
at its most banal. We've heard them before: they will say
anything.

Anyone in favor of an authoritarian state now that the Soviet
transnational empire is crumbling must grab the idea of the
nation and hold on for dear life: there is no better justification
for maintaining the status quo. That the Communist authoritarian state can easily be refashioned into a nationalist authoritarian state is obvious from the ease with which the
opposite process took place when the communists seized power.
And since the traditions, structures, and technology of a police
state are still very much in place, even a hardened democrat
may be tempted to find out more than he need know about his
faithful flock.

Even a Christian-national-right-of-center-conservative government must eventually formulate a program. Eager yet haggard
and somewhat disgruntled faces. They're doing the best they
can, but the opposition and even the rank and file are dissatisfied. People are wrangling over who gets what job—it's
vanity-fair time—and the faithful expect to be rewarded. The
victorious newcomers are starting to understand the practical

philosophy of the men they condemned and cashiered—to understand and follow it.

It is not clear what exactly, what political tradition, the people who call themselves conservative in East-Central Europe intend to conserve. If not the Kádár regime, then what? The Horthy regime? Or a right-wing tradition stylized into continuity and put in place by the personnel and power politics left over from state socialism?

The historical consciousness of East-Central Europe is gradually rehabilitating its pre-1945 politicians—Piłsudski, Tisza, Antonescu—and their politics with them. After homage comes justification. If communists are bad, anticommunists are good. And anyone with an ounce of taste refrains from bringing up fascism. Point out that Hungarians who went along with—or enthusiastically collaborated with—Nazi Germany were fascists, and the newly baked radical right tells you in increasingly petulant tones that you are talking liberal-communist, leftist-zionist poppycock.

An aggressive nationalist construct may well take shape alongside the right-wing parties, something like the Front National in France or the Republikaner in Germany. There the major right-wing parties are at pains to dissociate themselves from such groups, but in Hungary the new right has not quite come to grips with what it means to be a conservative in a parliamentary democracy. A year ago the right wing didn't even know it *was* a right wing; it still saw itself as the democratic opposition. Now it is nervously learning its new role.

The right wing is an amalgamation and hasn't yet split into factions. Its radicals haven't yet united into a movement; they prefer to work within the governmental coalition parties, especially as the leadership is careful not to criticize them in public. Far-right rhetoric tends to tread cautiously, within limits, all hints and figures of speech, until one day uniforms and jackboots appear on the streets and windowpanes begin to shatter.

Is there a tendency towards a renaissance of the radical right east of the former Iron Curtain? Are the demagogues who pop up now and again capable of putting together a movement, and could such a movement take over a government or system? Can Eastern Europe, so recently liberated from Communism, be swinging in the direction of radical nationalism?

I don't believe the East European pendulum has enough momentum in it to enable right-wing radicals to clear the political terrain and establish an authoritarian regime. I don't believe, therefore, that radical right tendencies can solidify into a fascist system. Nor do I believe that the bulk of my fellow citizens would welcome a shift in the authoritarian direction. Their democratic energy and political acumen have developed considerably in the past year. They need not fear neofascist ravings.

Another reason I am optimistic is that, except in Romania, the turn to democracy has claimed no human lives, that is, our region is not inherently bloodthirsty. And then, almost nowhere have extremists received a majority of the vote. East Europeans have been battered too often: they want centrist leaders, well-trodden paths; they won't follow upstart adventurers. It also helps to recall that ringleaders and would-be ringleaders don't mix. Anyone who wants to be a dictator in today's Eastern Europe can count on rivals, and rival mafiosi tend to cancel one another out.

If the right radicals do infiltrate the political center from the sidelines, that center will lose support from the greatest source of hope for the continent's eastern half: the continent's western half. No beggar is particularly pleasant to begin with, but a beggar spouting radical right inanities is more likely than most to be ignored.

East-European fascism was satellite fascism; it couldn't have existed without a major fascist power behind it. Take that away, and you take away the confidence of the few remaining fascists to stand up against the democratic majority, the parliamentary rules of the game, and Western public opinion. National fundamentalists have a hard time reconciling their cant with the logic of democracy, yet they don't dare repudiate that logic openly. In the long run the stubborn islands of dictatorship left in today's Europe are doomed to failure.

Many fear a return of dictatorship in an altered form. The only way we can learn what high-sounding words really mean is to live them on a day-to-day basis and to watch the mouths that pronounce them. We once mastered communist parlance; now we're becoming fluent in the Christian-national dialect. Both raise the state or, rather, the idea of the state above the individual. No observant citizen can be certain that choices are now made more often on the basis of merit than they were in previous years: ideological fidelity still takes precedence over technical competence.

The new system is by no means inimical to the less conspicuous representatives of the former regime, and the ruling parties have their share of them: people who find it easier to lick their wounds with a little power today than to hold off for more power tomorrow. Which is not to say that the opposition parties are completely devoid of them either. The change in regime inevitably introduced a bit of intellectual confusion—

half-baked pseudo-ideas from hither and yon, the kind of arbitrary drivel that an experienced conservative regime would have filtered out on the spot but that the new men second out of sheer cussedness.

People lacking professional reputation and political experience—older beginners—take undue offense at criticism and hide their anxieties by showing in no uncertain terms that they are in power. And then there is the pomp that comes with power. The day they take office is a red-letter day in the history of the nation: it means more than a new administration; it means a new outlook on the world, the glad tidings of a completely new system.

But there always have been and always will be competent, hard-working government officials who do their jobs as best as circumstances allow. Some even make important contributions. They will attack the opposition, of course, but in the ensuing debate they will clarify their own position, keeping, we hope, to a responsible, self-disciplined middle road. They don't need to be brilliant; they just need to steer clear of rash policies.

When I observe the way Hungary is developing internally, the first thing I see is the formation of a constitutional state based on the rule of law, a state that has not yet infringed upon its citizens' human rights and seems unlikely to do so in the near future.

Even though the situation is critical, even though the government is dragging its feet over essential bills and the basic structures are still more or less as we inherited them from state socialism, the economy shows signs of life and private initiative is expanding. The balance of trade is turning in our favor; hard currency deposits by Hungarians in Hungarian banks are

up; the gap between official and black-market prices is closing. Confidence in Hungary is growing, as is Hungary's self-
confidence, and deservedly so.

Hungary is a vital country which, its passionate polemics
and occasionally strong words notwithstanding, has defended
its interests in a nonviolent manner and done so with such
success that the major social changes which have taken place
over the past few months have, I repeat, cost not a single human
life. Passions soar, enemies insult one another right and left;
even people of the same camp and stamp wave swords in one
another's faces. I see much of it as playacting, even clowning.
Of all the East-Central European countries only Hungary has
succeeded in setting up a Western-style bipartite (conservative
vs. liberal) political structure capable of providing its citizenry
with a say in the government. Or, to be more precise, half its
citizenry, because the other half is bored with—or perhaps
doesn't quite yet understand—parliamentary procedure and can
see nothing more than that prices are rising week by week.

As a liberal I am not particularly happy about the inroads
made by the right; I do not enjoy the new kitsch any more
than I enjoyed the old; I am sorry to find the conservative
imagination so lacking in creativity. Yet I try to place our shift
to the right in the context of the entire region.

If Yalta is over and done with, if East Germany is a thing of
the past, if the Soviet Union is coming apart at the seams, if
the Slovenes and Slovaks can dream of an independent state
along with the Lithuanians and Armenians, then why should
our place on the geopolitical map be immutable? If the Iron
Curtain is no longer sacred, why should any line drawn by
politicians on the map be sacred?

Parallel to the move towards West European integration, the continent's eastern, post-Communist half is undergoing a major ethnic, religious, and national renaissance. The Soviet empire's East-bloc rhetoric stood in its way until recently, but now that the rhetoric and the bloc (and eventually perhaps the Union itself) have come to an end, nothing would seem to prevent all Eastern Europe—to the Urals and beyond—from reentering the world arena as a string of fervently nationalistic nation-states. Of course they will thereby inherit the fate of all nation-states in their part of the world: they will have trouble with national minorities, which will have been cut off from the mother country, or with the majority nation, which will blame its inability to create a homogeneous entity on what it perceives as minority separatism. Nation-states seeking homogeneity do not wish to recognize the fact that even they are multinational, multicultural in nature. To avoid a dispassionate appraisal of the situation they come up with reasons for being offended and mistrustful. Vague yet ardently defended identities emerge out of nowhere, every petulant new participant in the drama brandishing a list of long repressed grudges.

Most of these newly vocal, politically active groups define themselves with respect to one another, that is, their identity comes from pitting themselves staunchly, obstinately against neighboring nations or minorities. Hence the outside world tends to regard them as feuding twins, whose conflicts are tragic enough up close but absurd from a distance.

The majority nation cannot understand why the minority shows no desire to assimilate. Don't they like us? Maybe they think they're different. You mean they expect us to make the first move? Well, if they don't want to be like us, if they insist on talking their own language, if they've got a thing about their customs, if they feel they don't belong, if they keep arguing with us, if they hate us so, then why don't they pack up and leave? The impatient majority, which called for the speediest possible assimilation, now calls for the speediest possible dis-similation: Out! The result could in principle be a kind of chain reaction, each minority that breaks away and forms its own majority provoking a minority within it and thus stirring up feelings of national consciousness on both sides to murderous intensity.

All the countries in our region are multinational: Hungary, whose territory was reduced by a third after World War I, to a lesser extent; Hungary's neighbors, who gained the territory Hungary lost, to a greater extent. Anyone who thinks exclu-sively in terms of a nation-state is doomed to endless clashes with the area's ethnic realities, a fact easier to grasp from the vantage point of the loser than from the vantage point of the victor. In an ethnically mixed region nationalists look to history for support: their goal is to prove that their forefathers were first to arrive in the land in question or first to seize it from the first recorded inhabitants; the older they can make their col-lective self appear, the better. Odd, isn't it? People basing their public image on who first grabbed the land they live on—not to mention writers ready to spin self-justificatory myths out of the most meager of facts.

Once nationalists catch the fundamentalist fever, they have a hard time shaking it off. The psychosis of collective resentment takes over to such an extent that its victims perceive everything as an affront to their national pride. "I told you so!" they shout, gloating over the conviction that the other national or ethnic community is plotting to do them in.

The national fundamentalist is leery of logic; he answers questions that differ from the ones he is asked; he only pretends to carry on a dialogue. There is no way to find a common language with him, because he places his nationalist concerns above fair play. Not only does he fail to understand his interlocutors, he has no wish to understand them, he's afraid to understand them: it might upset his self-assurance.

Mature nations have put flaming egocentrism behind them; young nations have yet to do so. The symptoms are easy to recognize: ordinary people suddenly puff up with a belief in their unique mission, often just after a successful demagogue (and potential dictator) has appeared on the scene, dazzling them with his megalomaniacal dream.

The large European nations have sown their wild oats: each of them once believed—though believes no more—in its destiny to unite and gain dominion over the entire region. Then came the small nations' turn. Small nations are not so meek as you might think, not among themselves at least. Anything they deemed worthy of annexation they tried to annex; anyone they deemed worthy of betrayal they tried to betray.

History in twentieth-century Eastern Europe is a grim affair consisting of one invasion after another (with the collusion of the great powers) and of officially sanctioned discrimination against minorities. The extermination of two-thirds of European Jewry was not entirely the Germans' handiwork: local fascist movements did their share. Majority and minority seemed to be living in harmony when suddenly a series of lynchings, pogroms, and deportations broke out. True, there were instances of one nation showing solidarity with another, one nation defending another's sovereignty, and they deserve to be celebrated. Every rescue attempt, every offer of asylum, every instance of support should be remembered and kept alive. But more often than not the strategic options available led to unfortunate decisions, decisions that the underdevelopment of political sovereignty in the area between Germany and Russia may explain but in no way justify.

A country without political sovereignty is a satellite. A satellite has no responsibility or, rather, it shifts its responsibility onto someone else: its boss, its patron, the superpower that has undertaken to represent its interests. As a result, what the Germans call *Vergangenheitsbewältigung,* "coming to grips with one's past," is extremely difficult here.

Nations here are unable to take a long, critical look at certain periods in their history. Self-justification is part and parcel of national self-consciousness, especially when the nation in question feels it has been slighted. And what nation in our region does not?

Various forms of European fascism encouraged national claims that in the nature of things were part truth and part delirium. For example, German expansion on the eve of the Second World War gave Slovaks and Croats an opportunity to form independent states. It being the misfortune of the impatient latecomer to have to accept support from wherever it is proffered, these minority nations used the threat of war to disengage themselves from the majority nations with which they had been living in a nation-state and to realize their—autonomist? separatist?—ambitions.

The cult of the nation-state must not blind us to the issue of smaller territories and their sovereignty. Nothing can be more important for the democratization process in Eastern Europe than the independence of local governments from the centers of power, the representatives of the majority, the nation-state. Nationalist solidarity, like its communist counterpart, is inimical to territorial autonomy.

No state-sanctioned borders are going to stop people from wanting to govern themselves. Nor is it possible anymore to deny minorities territorial autonomy and confederative covenants: they are too much a part of the unique and uniquely complex relations among the peoples living in our region. From Karabakh to Kosovo, from Székelyföld to southern Slovakia claims for local government and self-determination are in the air, claims with a definite immediacy about them. The mirage of confederation is on the horizon, and historical border changes are the order of the day.

The idea of a territorial state is more realistic than the idea of a single-nation, single-language state. It allows for human reality, which—made up, as it is, of individuals—is by nature diverse. There is no region or town of any size that is not multicultural.

Individuals have rights because they exist in time and space. They are registered at birth in a community, and when they come of age, the community grants them certain civil rights. The language they speak, the nationality they avow, the faith they profess is their business. Identifying the essence of a political state with one language community or another was an error propagated in the nineteenth century by overenthusiastic literati tainted by a lust for power. State nationalism—that is, the idea of a language-based national unit—is in constant conflict with ethnic and territorial reality. Language-based nation-states tend to exclude all those who speak other languages;

territory-based political states accept Babel-like diversity and grant all citizens equal rights.

One by one the myriad nations and nationalities of Eastern Europe are coming into their own. None can be silenced much longer. Every country in our region, for example, has millions of Gypsies. Little has been said of them until recently; now they are speaking for themselves. One by one the taboos are falling. This is a time for speaking out. New definitions of East European identity can be expected on a regular basis.

The criteria that hold for behavior among individuals hold for behavior among nationalities as well: what one people does to another determines the next stage in their relationship no less than what one person does to another. If one nationality commits a crime against another, it remains a crime: it cannot be glossed over or denied; it can only be expiated.

Every mass grave will be opened, every secret document made public, every atrocity called by its name.

Granted, the newly existing autonomies are tussling with one another, haggling with one another, but neighborly relations need not preclude candid communication. What is needed is a relatively unbiased third party, an independent perspective, a justice of the peace or moral magistrate to arbitrate among them, lacking as they do any court of appeals and given the failure of international organizations to keep local disputes from escalating. We must pay close attention to the evolution of democracy in Europe as a whole and Eastern Europe in particular, using one and the same thermometer to measure hate and tolerance across the continent. We need regular opinion polls to give a picture of the continent's mentality and enable Europeans to define their own positions in full cognizance of their neighbors'.

Nothing is more dangerous than cold, secretive, abstract, ideological hatred, system-bound hatred couched in erudite jargon. Ideological hatred can be measured by a content analysis of relevant texts compared on a country-by-country or target-by-target basis. We might thus trace the transition from democratic nationalism to fascistoid nationalism.

It makes sense for the European Community to accept new member states in accordance with the degree to which they meet European norms of human and civil rights, respecting the freedom of their citizens, minorities, and neighbors, respecting human integrity as a whole. This is a strategy to bring them in line with Western political democracy. Public opinion carries great weight in Europe. No regime in our part of the world can expect to last if it regularly, openly violates the laws that safeguard its citizens' rights. The criterion of human rights must be introduced both as a part of public policy and as a measure of economic integration. The map of world hunger shows that wherever laws protecting human rights are respected, people's stomachs are full; hunger reigns only in countries where a principle reigns, a principle higher than the freedom of the individual.

If the West has taken to stimulating democracy in our region by awarding or withholding support on the basis of its progress, it does so to promote West European security as much as East European economic development. To ensure against East Europeans slipping back to a Communist system or shifting to a nationalist one-party system (even if maintaining the veneer of a multiparty state), West Europeans have made the conditions for step-by-step integration perfectly clear.

We have an enormous amount to learn at once: we must learn parliamentary democracy and everything that goes with it; we must learn the dicipline of the ruling party and the discipline of the opposition. None of this is cut-and-dried, and the chance of a slip-up is always present. But so are the means to correct it.

As long as there is a universal system of values, there is a basis for reconciliation. Until recently the problem was the dictatorship of the communist minority; the new problem is the dictatorship of the nationalist majority. Concentration of power would appear to be endemic to the countries of Eastern Europe. We can therefore expect an outbreak of national, authoritarian movements, though the democratic, civil-rights movements will of course maintain their ties with one another. Their cause benefits from the transnational values they share and the solidarity that comes of their dissident pasts. The democratic opposition movement was the only force in postwar Eastern Europe to recognize publicly that we are allies in our own freedom.

With the dissolution of the empire we have become a haven for stray hatreds. The remaking of the political map of East-Central Europe and the shift in its cast of characters will continue to produce conflicts among its states, nations, republics, majorities, and minorities in all their profusion and combinations. Independent international advisory panels now intervene in the case of ecological conflicts, and the Red Cross is always available if blood should flow. Wouldn't it make more sense, though, to take preventive measures and avert the flow of blood?

1990

The Gallows Enters the Museum

Praise be to the Constitutional Court! Hungary has put an end to legalized murder, the death penalty. From now on only murderers—criminals, that is—will kill their fellowmen; non-criminals will have no need or excuse to do so.

The Council of Europe was right to declare the rejection of homicide (at least in times of peace and within the sovereignty of the state) a criterion of civilized rule, and the government of Hungary was right to turn to the Constitutional Court rather than Parliament when it decided to accept the Council's condition for membership.

Why is the abolition of capital punishment a criterion of civilized rule and the antithesis of barbarism? Because civilized rule, in its wisdom, recognizes that within one and the same species—the human species—no preordained moral superiority or inferiority between judge and judged does or can exist. A judgment expresses an opinion, a prejudice; in other words, it is relative. An execution is absolute. The only truth that can exist between one human being and another is relative.

Judeo-Christian metaphysical democracy, which refuses to recognize any divinely derived hierarchy among humans, regards individuals as inherently equal. Hence no person is the master of any other person in the way a person may be the master of an animal (which members of our civilization still feel entitled to kill).

No person is the master of any other person, nor can one person be the absolute slave of another—absolute in the sense that he can take the other's life. One of the functions of the state is legal intimidation: the state is the institution empowered to threaten potential offenders with punishment, physical confinement, loss of liberty. That is, force. But if the state can threaten them with death as well, it can easily overstep its bounds and encroach upon the freedom of the individual.

If we accept the fact that every piece of evidence, every testimony, every moral position is contingent upon a given point in time, then we must also accept the fact that the absolute and irreversible nature of the death penalty is incompatible with the relative, reversible nature of human judgment.

It was not enough to pass a law stipulating that political offenders could no longer be hanged while common criminals could. Not only because there were numerous instances of "politicals" prosecuted by their enemies as common criminals but also because introducing an exception to the rule implies that the rule itself lacks hard-and-fast criteria and that who may be sentenced to death and who may not is determined less by justice than by power politics. Moreover, not every homicide is punished by death, so the decision of which one shall be and which one shall not is bound to be arbitrary.

An eye for an eye? A life for a life? But the *victim* isn't taking revenge on his murderer; it's somebody else, a third person, who was innocent until he delivered the sentence and is now implicated in a murder. You can't pay a judge to put an execution on his conscience. Can you order a second person to murder a third? No one has the superhuman insight to know the punishment he has inflicted when he hands down the severe decree, the final decree.

Wherever there is a death penalty, there are people sentenced to death. One day they are executed for one reason, the next day for another. The sentence can be justified in all kinds of ways and made to fit the most varied ideologies. The very existence of the institution is a temptation.

If we could make a film showing all the death sentences delivered in Hungary during the twentieth century, if we could watch all the parties involved, look the accused and accusers in the eye, in how many cases would today's morality accept yesterday's judgments?

Since in principle every sentence can be wrong and since a prisoner can leave a prison but a corpse cannot leave a coffin, no punishment makes sense unless it is continually subject to scrutiny and can be changed as the evidence in the case and the interpretation of the evidence change. The door to the house of the law must not only be the same for everyone; it must open out as well as in.

I feel proud that in 1990 Hungary joined the ranks of civilized nations where homicide is forbidden outright and nothing is more sacred than a human life; where murder is not punished by murder, and the murder rate is lower than in countries where murderers know they may be executed.

There is no doubt that the killing spirit is catching, but so is the spirit of not killing. It might even reach the army and the butcher's block.

1990

Something Is Over

If everything around us is changing, we must be changing too.

Literature as we knew it under socialism—that is, literature as a national institution—has ceased to exist. Gone are our cheap books: the state no longer has an interest in whether its citizens read what its writers have to say. We writers are no longer high priests, but we are no longer heretics either. Nor was political dissent ever really the domain of literature proper: when criticism can be heard in parliament or read in the dailies, it does not need to play hide-and-seek between the covers.

Besides, political statements as such have lost their ability to shock. Indifference is a great leveler. And when it comes to the most heated controversies of the day, writers are suddenly rank amateurs. Writing is a less serious profession than it was; it is more a hobby, a pastime, a sport. Priests have reclaimed their prerogative to speak on exalted topics, and politicians are fed grandiloquent formulas by speechwriters. Writers have no more reason to wax lofty. In a liberal democracy our fellow citizens do not need our spiritual guidance. What they need are good books.

Under state socialism the writer performed a positive or negative function, while in bourgeois society the writer is a private individual capable of providing certain information. And—insofar as we are actually living in a liberal democracy —what writers write is their business and their business alone. If there is little interest in what they have to say, they can publish it themselves in one or two thousand copies. A year or two after the big change, writers are still fretting over whether they serve a purpose, fill a need. They have begun to suspect they are passé. The money is gone; the power is gone. The market has not yet found a way to make them profitable; the state no longer wants them.

The socialist state needed them if they didn't kick up too much of a fuss. The state maintained its own culture, which consisted of books passed by its censor, but that culture was supplemented by an uncensored one. Even today the state has money to subsidize a culture more or less loyal to itself; the culture it does not perceive as loyal it leaves to its own devices, that is, to the private economy. Gone are the days when writers could count on living off one book a year for the rest of their lives. Many are unemployed. This is a time of trial. Writers must find a way to combine literature with other forms of activity and accept the idea that they need not stick to one profession all their lives.

Books have become more expensive, readers less solvent. Trash is the rage. People not only have less money for books; they have less time for books. Literature is occupying less and less space in our lives. Only now, in retrospect, can we see this clearly: an age in the history of literature has come to an end.

Literature has sunk to the lowest rung on the institutional ladder. The national associations or unions of writers—for long, bastions of the institutionalization of literature—are on the verge of splintering into interest groups. The republic of literature as a body of normative spiritual values is a thing of the past.

Publishing is going through the same crisis as the other branches of the economy. Literature shares in the new poverty. Still, I feel that the period of rising book prices and falling incomes is a transitional one and that literature will come out of it intact. We can be confident of the emergence, a few years hence, of a stronger middle class that has not lost its taste for literature. Eventually cheaper technology and rising incomes will take care of the problem.

Until then, however, seven lean years. Only the determination of a monk will keep a life's work going, and only the most hardened professionals among us—and hardened amateurs—will be able to write their way through the famine. Many will simply return to earning their keep by means of one intellectual endeavor or another and writing on the side. Those who stick it out will have to look to private benefactors for support—agencies of civic redistribution, like charities or foundations.

Two other institutions will help to keep literature alive. One is the press. Some newspapers have disappeared, but others are springing up to take their place, and the print and broadcast media both consume enormous amounts of text. Moreover, by the time readers have plowed their way through the headlines, they may well be thirsting for the relief provided by a writer's more permanent "news." There is a need for something more than the politician's exposition of a party platform or commentary on it by a self-proclaimed independent; there is a need for thoughtful, personal views, for points of reference in today's terrain of shaken values. There are issues that need to be addressed by names, reputations, well-formulated texts. The power of the word is still very much alive, and there is a market for advice. The more mobile and unsettled a population is, the more it needs serious, well-considered opinions.

The second institution that will help is international publishing. Western Europe is experiencing a wave of interest in the rest of Europe and in the rest of the world. National egotism is far from dead, but it cannot stop people from thinking, and it is not yet considered a quality worthy of celebration. To the east of the former Iron Curtain, however, the outburst of national sentiment, which played so crucial a role in the breakup of what used to be called the Soviet bloc or socialist world, has considerably weakened the bonds—and with them the once ritualistic cultural exchanges—among members of what used to be called Comecon. As a result there has been little incentive to establish a true exchange of ideas on the East-Central European front. Here publishing has been a negative force: its malady—or, as bleaker seers would have it, its collapse—prevents our books from becoming bestsellers in our own part of the world.

Writers in our part of the world and century have overrated their importance, becoming propagandists, priests, proclaiming this or that principle, railing against the demon of the day, playing the spiritual leader. The time has come to change all that. State socialism was so dependent on ideology that it could not survive without the cooperation of a loyal intelligentsia;

now the chapter of extraliterary commitment is closed. Writers are no longer required to foist beside-the-point attitudes on their readers, to go outside their craft and crossbreed literature with something that has little to do with it. There is always a quasi-moral inducement to crossbreeding literature with something else, and some writers feel they can't do without it. They picture themselves arriving in the nick of time, only moments before the ultimate catastrophe, and saving . . . what *do* they plan to save?

My twentieth century began the year Hitler took power: I was born in 1933.

Our century has been characterized by the view on the part of numerous radicals that it is both possible and desirable to take power by the most expedient means—by force, if necessary—and hold onto it for dear life. People and words traveled back and forth between nationalist and socialist revolutions, and the path of many an intellectual led from one to the other. The marriage between politics and literature has been an uneasy one in all this, never quite fusing, yet never entirely separate. Moreover, the twentieth century has brought politics into the home, the bedroom, the telephone, the brain. Both fascism and communism defended their states by reaching into our cupboards for manuscripts. It is in our interest to question any principle that authorizes a state to bully.

Dictatorships do not let their citizens forget politics; they relentlessly etch its tedious stimuli into our brains. Consequently no one can be naive and everyone must be vigilant. And because the state has its bias, the opposition has *its* bias. Even people who try to opt out, to find a small, safe corner for themselves and keep from being picked on, have a bias. Pro or con, impulse and anguish skew narration.

I see an inquisitive light in people's eyes: they want to know how things stand; they want explanations. The man in the street is less gullible than he was three years ago; he's got a lot more savvy, the savvy that comes of bitter experience. There is no political afterlife; the here and now is everything. You are what you are, not what you could be if the system were different.

The system is social-nationalist capitalism, and it's here to stay. You can call it names or turn it to your advantage. Doubting Thomases are looking for values instead of killing one another: the new politics has produced not a single casualty. There will be more poverty at first—then less. There will be more armed robbery—then, in all likelihood, less. Bankers and intellectuals have started feeling a mutual attraction. Life is no longer an enigma: what you see is more or less what you get. And what you see is a fast-change act accompanied by the patter of a new rhetoric.

But the developments have also given rise to a new amnesia: many people feel they have had their pasts snatched from them. So much of what they learned turns out to have been hogwash. They are not looking forward to the future, though they are willing to put up with it. They may even grow to love it—just because it's there.

I expect good books to come of the outlook that will emerge once wounded senses of identity have had time to heal and today's people have had time to gain insight into the people of yesterday and the day before (bearing in mind our region's propensity for tragically complex human destinies and self-justifying skulduggery). If good literature does result, it will surely show the making of history to be absurd, though the history makers were perfectly sensible and well-intentioned, and their aspirations far from absurd. Now that the time has come for narratives and epics-in-dialogue, we must ask which prevails in literature: the logic of the dialogue or the logic of tribal prejudice. Shall we be able to turn our past (which public opinion still sees in fashionably ideological terms) into an epic? What are the major lessons of the twentieth century? The mere fact that we have survived it does not lend any sense to the adventure. And can one have a life that makes sense in a history that makes none?

The eighties have come to an end, and as we enter the mysterious nineties, we must keep in mind their great riddle: Are we in a position to celebrate the second millennium, grateful for being, for being able to be, for holding our ground in this vale of tears and fallibility where we beguile or bore our God according to our moods and lights?

The twentieth century is coming to an end. It has been a century of aggression and irresponsibility. Its follies, its cataclysmic follies stream out of books and mass graves. No writer, no politician, no public figure is innocent. No one may level accusations, but no one is spared remorse. Remorse, the consciousness of guilt, goes hand in hand with responsibility. Shouldering responsibility for the future means shouldering responsibility for the past. Weak men take the places of weak men.

What did the lack of responsibility consist of? The bloating of thin-skinned collective egos. What did it lead to? Wars and dictatorships. One of the collective egos would take to expanding aggressively and self-righteously, wounding its neighbors' sensibilities, claiming the right to rule, sullying air and water, and bombing perfidiously—while explaining away gas chambers and labor camps with winsome arguments and proclaiming its supremacy on the basis of various world-historical or world-geographical missions.

All my arguments can be torn to pieces, I know, but I have a very personal disease: I am an optimist. Why? I see a number of determined individuals working hard to make this country work, to put it in the hands not of tricksters and con men but of movers and shakers (this is their time and the time for the foundations that support them). I see fewer cowed subjects waiting for the king to provide. The government has made considerable progress if it has learned to ban less. And it has. All things considered, I feel we have less reason to fear than we had last year at this time.

The dour anxiety so characteristic of the citizen of the socialist state is still an integral element of the post-communist citizen, but its causes have changed. People feel obliged to take an alarmist view of things. Everything can be talked about openly now, of course, and because the more dramatic the view the more attention it attracts, there are those who have turned scare tactics to their advantage. Yet even people who paint the most apocalyptic pictures on their walls in the dead of night go to work the next morning. And since more and more aspire to running their own lives and bad work is acquiring a bad name, the work they do is actually quite decent.

The author of these lines, fearing neither despotism nor

civil war, is guilty of heinous sobriety and patent complicity with the majority. His watchword being Trot Rather than Gallop or Ditch, he sees no grounds for hysteria, no reason to jump ship.

1991

More Than Nothing: The Role of the Intellectual in a Changing Europe

(Excerpts from the Inaugural Lecture for the Conference of German University Chancellors, Sankt Paulus Kirche, Frankfurt, 28 April 1991)

People are expected to serve noble causes. Of causes there is no end, and we tend to regard our own as noble and other people's as ignoble. Which leads your humble servant to muse, "What cause do I serve?" The customary answers—culture or society, church or state, humanity or nation, business firm or political party, the integrity of science or the autonomy of art—are all well and good, but since one can serve any number of masters (loyalty being an infinitely expandable concept), the simplest thing for me to say is, "I serve no one." Not even myself. Am I serving my wife when I carry her suitcase? Am I serving my son when I play bear with him? Am I serving my guests when I wine and dine them? Am I serving my publisher when I hand in a manuscript? No. These activities are an integral part of living together: we do what can reasonably be expected of us, we take pleasure in it, and others pay us back in kind. Whom do I serve when I lift my pen and set it down on a sheet of paper? Who is served by an idea or a question? A sentence—this sentence—is because it wishes to be.

If I refuse to serve—if at most I cooperate—what am I good for? Merely to be? To partake in the sometimes heavenly, sometimes hellish blessings of existence? To acknowledge my birth by keeping myself alive? To make ready for the time when I am good for nothing? People don't come with instruction manuals. If they aren't created to serve a cause, if they don't do what they do for the sake of posterity or an afterlife, if they have no preordained obligations, then they are fully responsible for their own acts! They must determine—improvise, one might say—their obligations for themselves; they must set their own agendas; they must provide a more or less personal rationale for each decision they take. And that rationale is as central to their existence as the loves of their life or the tools of their trade. Moreover, internal obligations grow as external obligations shrink, the critical mind (the intellectual's chief tool) corroding the external plan and allowing the contours of an internal plan to emerge.

Why not start at zero? Everything that is is more than nothing. Even an obituary can give life: it enriches our emotional landscape, makes us grateful for one more day, helps us to see life as something given to us, not something coming to us. For we are worthless creatures and have nothing whatever coming to us. The fact that we emerge from nothing and return to nothing, the fact that we are alive is in itself a gift, a reciprocal gift, a gift of mutual gain, because in life as in love, giving is receiving. We cannot make a clear-cut distinction between ourselves and those near to us. We establish a symbiotic relationship with our environment in such a way as to merit at least a mental stroll through the realm of the end-in-itself, and as we stroll, we indulge in the idea of having a self-contained purpose. If dust we are and unto dust we shall return, if such is our only trajectory, if we are made in God's image and thus meant to be as perfect as our Heavenly Father, then let us be unique and like unto Him who made us. Life is a form that becomes visible only with the passing of time and the presence of someone desiring to behold it. The challenge is to create a work out of the limited time we are given.

Our job is to live, and to live is to live together. We live together in the classroom and the dining room, in the hospital and the air-raid shelter, in the swimming pool and in bed. We miss one another and make sacrifices for one another, though when we grow up and move apart, we lose sight of one another. Nor do we need to be together all the time: solitude has its merits. Where do old alliances go? Into the sack of things past, the ego's timeless chronology. We are for ourselves and one another as animals are and the heavenly bodies.

Life from this standpoint is an arbitrary gift and should therefore be appreciated as it stands. If we proceed from the assumption that the end can come at any moment, history begins anew for every individual every day, though most people grow more defined, confined, and calcified in what is unremitting agony. The more rigid, the more unbending one is, the more mortal one is. Taking a shape, accepting a mold, moving in a single direction—all mean coming to nought. Yet we do have a certain freedom to choose how we cover the short stretch allotted us: there are a variety of paths available.

As attentive as we are to our own comforts and impulses, as accustomed as we are to looking after ourselves and even others, we know that at any moment we can have a stroke or a car accident, we can be done in by business failure or heart failure, by a family tragedy or a pistol shot. It follows that the novels we write with our lives may end today or any day. Just being able to open our eyes is a gift.

Honoring the here and now goes against the transcendental. I am not attracted by religious or scientific futurism; I do not believe the future is more radiant than the present. The idea of a more tolerant approach to life is spreading quietly: integration and compassion are taking the place of isolation and expulsion. I also sense a new sincerity, something beyond science and religion, beyond politics and public relations. The core of that sincerity lies in an awareness of death. The place where we are most likely to confront our morality is art. The artist knows a story has more than a beginning; the artist knows a story has an end.

If this view of life focuses on the here and now, it is simply because the here and now is where the challenge lies. Yesterday cannot remedy today; tomorrow's noble goal is no excuse for today's crime. What counts is what you do now. If you are traveling on a train or bathing your child, that is your creative work for the moment.

Everyone wants to be an artist: everyone writes, draws, plays an instrument, indulges in some kind of intellectual or spiritual luxury; everyone gives both imagination and memory a workout; everyone has hidden concerns. Every graybeard retains a nook of childlike innocence, and we all soar out of ourselves occasionally and enjoy transforming the reality around us. This cerebral rambling, this internal cinema takes up a good deal of our time; it runs from the cradle to the grave, oblivious even to hardening of the arteries. In fact, we devote more time to it than to the conscious and conscientious lifelong work we do in connection with the outer world. It is the opposite of goal-oriented activity, incorporating elements of art and play, and if we add our night- and daydreams to it, it turns out to occupy the greater part of our lives.

Although writers and professors and actors and historians have become leading figures in the new democracies, I don't think intellectuals wish to make a policy of excluding politicians and businessmen, revolutionaries and secret service men, civil servants and clergymen. The intelligentsia could learn these people's professions, but they would only be disguises for its own: the profession of understanding. That is why I don't think the intelligentsia is interested in direct political or economic power. It will keep to its natural medium and the power of the word, the image, the symbol.

If intellectuals have power, they must have a vocation as well. The intelligentsia is the keeper of legitimacies: it provides grounds for morality, argumentation for the law, exegesis for religion, allegories for ethics, and analysis for politics. In other words, intellectuals peddle clear consciences and guilty consciences. All people have cultural values to guide them and justify their existence, to help them believe they are in the right and what they do is good. Those values are in the hands of the intellectuals.

Most intellectuals want to multiply and fill the streets, spread their wares in the marketplace. They want to invade other people's books if only in a footnote; they want to be referred to, referred to more than their rivals. They know the value of sacrifice, having become slaves to competitive examinations and quantitative hierarchies early in life. They work long, hard hours, subordinating the emotional to the professional. If all goes well, they produce copious articles, attract disciples, found schools of thought. They sacrifice their lives for a name, the pettiest form of survival.

But our times call for knowledge that goes beyond these intellectuals' technical expertise; our times call for the knowledge of the initiate. Initiates care about nothing but the issue at hand. There is no discovery without passion, and these madmen are committed to what they do for its own sake, not for the fame it may bring. Careers are irrelevant to understanding. (A career does no harm, but it must not become a goal in itself.)

Intellectuals of the initiate type—*true* intellectuals, we might call them—are few in number. Perhaps they needn't be numerous. Groups of several dozen in major cities have sufficed to create all the short-lived intellectual golden ages the world has known.

Moreover, there is such a thing as an international intellectual elite, though its composition and contributions are not always apparent until after the fact. And because words influence people, there is such a thing as intellectual power—priest, prophet, and poet power—the power of individuals considered wise and therefore vested with authority. The burden of confidence weighs heavy on such individuals—on doctors, for instance. Their wisdom is their debt to the world, their duty; understanding is their profession. Sometimes it takes a naive soul to notice things others miss, and such people tend to be visionaries, too busy to worry about the prevailing course of events or their own skins. One way intellectuals communicate is by referring to the great names of the mythologies of their trade, the not-quite-of-this-world freaks of the spirit.

Where does the university come in? Well, teachers breed teachers, and if things go well, that means mature adults who can stand up to the jokes of fate, who under pressure do not renounce what they hold dear. Every adult is an idealist in a way. Adults know they have obligations, obligations they set for themselves. The opposite of the adult is the plastic person, the kind who assumes whatever shape happens to be advantageous. Plastic people are ready to change at a moment's notice. With a minimum of coaching, for instance, they can master a whole new vocabulary. They are like spare parts, easily interchangeable. That is what makes them so valuable. From burnt-out informer to shiny paragon in no time flat.

This is a dangerous period: words are falling into disrepute; everything is jumbled together—character hash, memory mush—and no one can take consolation anymore in the idea that things will change. What is, is.

Most people are surprised that nothing seems to be working out the way they thought it would: everything is chaotic, everything a mess, there's too much excitement, too much going on at once! Now someone has come along and predicted the chaos is over: we're in for harmony; history has come to an end. But then there's the problematic human race, a half-wild, half-domesticated species capable of anything. Though fully cognizant of the natural history of decline and decay, though fully aware of man's endless reserves of evil, I still say the people I admire most are idealists who are willing to make sacrifices for worthy goals and who feel they have a specific, personal mission in life, one they do not know in advance but decipher as they go along.

Universities transmit values. It is not enough for them to turn out apathetic specialists. The harm apathetic specialists can do far exceeds their potential for good. Think of the engineers and businessmen—upstanding citizens all—who place the most lethal weapons in the hands of any tyrant with the money to pay for them. Indifference, conformism, a lack of professional ideals, an impersonal readiness to do anybody's bidding as long as the technology is available—people have to be taught these things for major crimes against humanity to take place.

If by some strange quirk of fate I were to find myself on a podium, I would spend less time teaching my students the tricks of the trade than inculcating in them a feeling of personal responsibility. You have been entrusted with a life, I would tell them, and that makes you responsible for yourself and, in your person, for the whole of humanity. Responsibility has a way of popping up in front of you; all you have to do is recognize it. It is not enough to be a scholar; it is not enough to be an intellectual; it is not enough to follow a set of norms. The world does not owe you a living.

Nor is it enough to train specialists to satisfy the short-term demands of the market or the state: the university should serve as an antidote to the world.

We are swept along by the norms we learn, by ever more rigid professional roles, and find it increasingly difficult to assert the personal element. Universities are producing career-oriented intellectuals designed to fit reigning political clichés like off-the-peg jackets. Wholesale identification with a profession is crippling. Are you doing your job or is your job doing you? You are graded and typed while in school. A role can be an agenda, too. A plan, a prescription, a set of precepts, a strategy.

Art constitutes the day-to-day existence of the idealist: idealists do only what they respect; otherwise they refuse. "I refuse" is a morality in itself: we need not participate in anything we judge to be wrong. The time has come for personal responsibility to take the place of collective responsibility. The twenty-first century will be the century of carefully considered and consciously espoused personal responsibility.

The twentieth century was the century of collective crime and collective irresponsibility (or the call for collective responsibility), and all its lunacy began in books. Yes, intellectuals *are* responsible for what their contemporaries do. People are more than active beings, they are moral beings: they want the propriety of their acts confirmed; they do what they think right, what they are brought up to do, what enhances their spiritual profile. They do what they are told.

The social history of the intelligentsia consists entirely of a continuous jockeying for increased autonomy, because for the intellectual true power is freedom. If intellectual endeavor is to thrive, it must sever all ties with authority external to it. Pluralism provides the elbowroom necessary for maneuvering, and intellectuals are by definition the athletes of understanding.

Theirs is a creative understanding, one that accepts the contradictions of the Other and values his or her aesthetic complexity. No one can understand a person from above; viewing a person from a position of superiority leads to platitudes, to reductionist simplifications that make the person boring and have nothing to do with understanding.

We have turned into a world society: far-off catastrophes and wars or mere changes in fashion make it abundantly and immediately clear that we are dependent on humanity as a whole and humanity as a whole depends on us. Our lives can be affected by a clever lunatic whose artistic forte happens to be mass destruction, the destruction of foreigners and his own kind, mixed. We are affected by new collective identities that up and decide that they are incompatible with their neighbors and think nothing of killing to gain sway over them. In Eastern Europe these collective identities are particularly explosive. In their hysteria they feel surrounded by enemies and therefore in dire need of cleansing their ethnic-national-religious-linguistic-tribal ranks (a process that includes rewarding the politically loyal). While communist dictatorships wither on the vine, their internationalist ideology no longer viable, national dictatorships are blossoming.

Now that the big nations' bloc system—that is, a world order resting on the nuclear powder keg—is no more, the little nations (and nationalities) want their own way and, to some extent, the right to tell others what to do. They are restless; they take potshots at their neighbors and demand territorial autonomy. A minority turns majority, which then breaks up into more minorities, each insisting on its own voice. The continent is teeming with autonomies; dissolution fever has reached epidemic proportions. Only yesterday all talk was of unification, and people believed it was good. Now all talk is of breaking asunder, and people believe it is good. Both doctrines, the doctrine of unity and the doctrine of autonomy, are the work of people who write books. If things go on like this, anyone who fails to rage against his neighbor is liable to be accused of treason.

East Europeans did not drink in capitalism with their mother's milk; they had to learn it as adults. It is only natural that they should be unsure of themselves and thus suffer from wounded pride. Enter a band of mediocrities with their fists in the air. The hatred is there; it just needs someone to direct it.

Does the region recognize the latent fascism in all this? Sometimes it is not so latent. Anticommunist rhetoric is increasingly peppered with far-right clichés. Professional hate-mongers on the lookout for an international mafia are beginning to give their devil Jewish features, a revival that reeks of unfinished prewar business.

I see a special role for the intelligentsia, a new class that has proved its ability to live dangerously in our century. It played no mean part in the raving intolerance of our two collectivisms, providing theory, in the wings, for the vulgarizers and organizers on stage. "Bourgeois individualism" got low marks from the state intelligentsia, "the world bourgeoisie" even lower; provincialism swaggered. Much of the inflated moral indignation, indeed, much of the ideologies themselves stemmed from a lack of familiarity with foreign languages. Insecure egos found support in peremptory rhetoric. Both collectivisms banned genuine artists and promoted pseudo-intellectuals. Much as we would like to believe that these subservient sub-intelligentsias played themselves out during their bloody-kitsch heydays, we cannot be certain. How insane it would be if even now, as we rejoice over communism's death throes, they gave birth to a strapping anticommunist fascism.

———

Nationalism and socialism have lost their timeliness for Europe; Europe's future lies elsewhere. Their messages are more nostalgic than productive: if one side goes too far, it will turn into fascism; if the other goes too far, it will turn into communism. And because Europe not only attended their performances but—this being the twentieth century and thus a time of living theater— also took active part in them, I feel we can still use the notion of antipolitics. Antipolitics: the moral criticism of politics. Morality cannot be politics, but it can be politics' demon (in Socrates' sense of the word), its incubus, its bad conscience; it can be politics' dreamwork. The cynicism of antipolitics can keep us from being duped. The authorities may seem to be taking responsibility, but they will not pay for the harm they cause.

The exciting events accompanying the changes could only have been followed by a letdown. Transformation there was, but not transfiguration. Despondency in one corner, that morning-after feeling in the other. The same people lining up, though in different formations. Moreover, whole countries, whole regions can change uniforms as easily as individuals. Both the bird's-eye and cat's-eye views of the new line-ups and uniforms make grotesque sights. It goes without saying that, in terms of friendships and animosities and whom you can trust and whom you can't, people are the same. What modifications there are resemble those you make from one marriage to the next. After imposing liberation, the new system has imposed a new accommodation.

The keen observer will note that a new series of buzzwords has appeared on the scene. Why not, after all? Don't we want to learn languages quickly and easily and expose quasipluralist self-censorship?

Of course a pluralist intelligentsia too can share in illusions and forced silence. During the seventies and eighties, for instance, the author of these lines was struck by the reluctance among his West German conversation partners to picture a Europe that was no longer defined by the Iron Curtain, a Europe in which Germany's place in the balance of power was redefined. The experts labeled all such talk a pipe dream: the serious public was engrossed in debating the number of missiles to be maintained on German soil. But when the Hungarians opened their borders to the East Germans, the Wall came tumbling down —and with it an entire way of thinking. Suddenly our mutual dependence and responsibility were as clear as allegory.

Euphoria over the change in system stemmed from a genuine sense of liberation when the air came whooshing out of the imaginary collective ego as out of an old balloon. The keen observer will note, however, that there are new balloons on the market.

Looking backward, we must keep in mind that communist censorship did more than prohibit; it affirmed, affirmed all manner of things. Moreover, it did so in exalted tones and as often as not in the first-person plural. Even its first-person singular was essentially a first-person plural.

What the unsuspecting man in the street fails to see is that once more a common ego has started talking in the first-person plural. It may don the toga of independence, but it talks in terms of "we all." A clear statement of independence is not enough, nor even the sincere desire to put it into practice: good intentions alone do not ensure the creation of, say, good poetry.

State functionaries during the communist period had no idea how much their every move was conditioned by the state, how much the one-party-state, first-person-plural mentality had permeated their consciousness. Shifting to a nation-state, first-person-plural mentality does not take any great mental effort. Shifting from the first-person plural of the Soviet Empire, whose sole concern was to maintain its crumbling colonies, to, say, the first-person plural of North Ossetia is perfectly simple and would be perfectly fine—were it not for Ingush neighbors.

The entire East European region is pregnant with new autonomies ready to burst out into the world and show how unique they are, each—naturally—vying to be first among equals as well as among minorities. Until recently their aspirations were foiled by the Soviet Empire; now they are foiled by a neighboring nation or nationality. The majority foils the minority, the minority the majority. Roles may change, but the other party is always the troublemaker. *L'enfer, c'est les autres.* Hell is other people in the ethno-national context too.

Lost souls are seeking new support and loyalties but also new targets for their rancor, which has only grown with the hardships imposed by the post-Communist economy. Relations with the East have disintegrated more quickly than relations with the West can be established. If the eastern half of the continent is not to feel lost and succumb to hysteria, it must be offered the prospect of step-by-step integration into Europe in the foreseeable future, despite the relatively minor (yet all but inevitable) disadvantages involved. For the breakup to have meaning, there must be a reconstruction plan giving the countries that have seceded a space where they can be reintegrated.

The German model of national socialism cast an ominous shadow over my youth, the Russian model of a socialist world order over my adult years. What now? After these German and Russian models of socialism I can envisage many people wanting domestic, homegrown varieties free of foreign influence, small-scale national socialisms, predominantly state-run but with an admixture of private enterprise.

The new supervalue is a pure "we": loyal sons of the mother- or fatherland cannot imagine more congenial company than one another, and anyone who befouls his nest by protesting is a traitor and deserves to have his tongue cut out or be beaten to death. At least that is how most of the anonymous letter writers would have it.

Whether the authoritarian state with its intimidation tactics, its suppression of criticism, its habit of turning opposition into enemy, its buggings and hiring-firing games, its favoritism and nepotism, its tendency to siphon state funds into the pockets of business partners, its rush to reunite politics, culture, and the economy after only halfhearted attempts at making them autonomous, its revival of the one-party state, its reinterpretation of the common good as the good of the party or party faction, its unctuous exterior and mafia-tough core, its police-immune posses, its demagoguery of hatred, its anonymous death threats in letters and phone calls—whether the authoritarian state uses communist or fascist rhetoric is less interesting than whether it is in fact what we now have, whether all that has happened is that the flatterers and liars have regrouped. Most interesting of all is whether the large-scale experiment under way in the region will enable independent thinkers to take the place of their state-oriented predecessors.

The peoples of Central Europe are following the East Germans' progress with rapt attention. Will the East Germans become independent or second-class citizens in the new, unified Germany? How they fare after the capitalist shock treatment they are now undergoing will be a telling omen for us. After all, they are now part of the much coveted fold, enjoying not only the relative confidence of the thirty-five countries of Europe—the supercontinent that, broadly conceived, includes both Siberia and North America, reaching as it does from one coast of the Pacific to the other rather than merely from the Atlantic to the Urals—but also a certain intimate advantage vis-à-vis the old-boy networks of NATO and the European Community.

East German identity—if there ever was one—seems from the outside to have given way. But can those forty-five years be forgotten like the twelve that preceded them? Perhaps forgetting has become expedient again.

Germans living east of the Elbe seem to have placed themselves totally in the hands of Germans living west of the Elbe. Not only are their machines run-down; they themselves are run-down, their self-image impaired. Hard as it is to accept, liberation and collective self-deprecation can go hand in hand.

Hungarians, Poles, and Czechs have no rich Western uncle, but they do have a millennium of history in which communism was but a brief chapter. True, they played their part in that chapter, but they overcame it as Hungarians, Poles, and Czechs and thus emerged with their self-identity intact. The Germans' dilemma, as I see it, is whether to reject communism as an alien construct and claim it did not happen to them or to accept it as part of their history. The East Germans played their communist roles with no less devotion than the East Europeans, and the only way of proving that West Germans would not have done the same is to prove that the people living on the even-numbered side of the streets separated by the Wall differed radically in character from the people living on the odd-numbered side.

Communism, like national socialism, is a part of German history. Jettisoning chapters from a tradition is psychologically unsound.

During the seventies and eighties my impression was that the Germans had done more to confront their Second World War past than the Hungarians, a situation connected with, among other things, their having played a more active role and the Hungarians a more acquiescent role in the events. Last year a number of German journalists asked me whether I feared them, meaning the new enlarged Germany. No, I said. Germany may be powerful, but each individual German is as much the little man as any other mortal.

I was not particularly comforted to see the Germans put their national identity problem on ice, though I knew it would not remain there for long. Can what we in Eastern Europe call the national renaissance or nationalist upsurge circumvent Germany?

In the atmosphere of growing self-awareness following the fall of communism will the desire to reestablish continuity bring the Germany of the thirties back into fashion? Romantic commentators notwithstanding, Hitler's Germany had no more demons than other places, though it did have less autonomy. Because the validity of the goal went unquestioned, its radical implementation went unimpeded. The *Volk* accepted its leaders' project unthinkingly, worked hard, and followed directions loyally. Had the people been more slipshod, less thorough, they would not have caused nearly so much suffering.

As the twentieth century draws to a close, Germany—a liberal *Rechtsstaat* and the world's number-one export power—stands in the transnational forefront of Western-style democracies. Today's Germans are no longer the aggressive egoists or knights of irrationalism the world once saw in them. A large nation has been granted the opportunity to unite two civilizations, two human types in such a way as to avoid the subordination, liquidation, or even excoriation and humiliation of one by the other.

Uniting the two Europes in Germany is a paradigmatic challenge. It is logical that in the process all parties should examine their former selves and alter them accordingly.

What I would tell my students, then, is: Don't identify the responsible individualism of the twenty-first century with the numbing, consumer-driven mass individualism of the twentieth. You have nothing coming to you, I would tell them, nothing but the whole world, and your calling as students is to formulate a worldview based on your own, first-person experience.

Keep studying, I would tell them; keep rethinking things after you leave the university and for the rest of your lives. Only then you will be able to oppose tyranny.

Beware of abstractions and terminologies, I would say; pay close attention to everyone fate or inspiration puts in your path. The least you can do is make Europe an electronic network of distinct entities. Why? So it continues to exist. So we don't kill one another off.

And finally, I would dissuade students in the West from playing missionary in the East. Don't go too far, I would tell them, because the natives may get restless and boil you for dinner.

1991

Identity and Hysteria

The Serbs, like the Croats and the Slovenes, are asking the world to support a cause they believe is just. Indeed, each group believes its cause to be so profoundly just that it feels justified in threatening the world with a third world war should its demand for support go unheeded. Prophets are thus holding out the prospect of a great Armageddon.

The majority is happy in the rank and file of its nation or tribe: its sense of belonging is completely fulfilling. Nationalists *are* their nation from head to toe, and suddenly they can't tolerate living under the same roof with "those other people." National identity drives everything from the collective conscious ness: trade, laws, culture. The majority nation has no interest in dividing up assets and liabilities after the divorce. It goes on about a nation's right to autonomy, to self-determination, but has nothing to say about the rights of minority nations within the new majority's boundaries.

There are no pure principles—not even national autonomy,

not even territorial integrity. If you kill in the name of something, you kill in the name of an abstraction. Yugoslavia's territorial integrity is not sacrosanct, nor is the autonomy of its peoples. Nobody's autonomy is sacrosanct if it leads to persecution and oppression, if it violates human rights. Why should Croat autonomy be holier than Serb autonomy? Or Serb autonomy be holier than Croat or Albanian autonomy? If my right to self-determination and your right to self-determination clash, then neither is self-evident. The only higher principle is compromise: not fighting, not hurting, not killing.

The country cannot be divided; the problem cannot be solved. Everyone backs the breakup and everyone claims the spoils, but no one wants to assume the debts. Who will decide? Arms won't help. Not even the Serbs have enough arms to win: the Yugoslav Army is in a bad way.

During the Second World War the Serbs killed four hundred thousand Croats; the Croats killed many more Serbs, let alone Jews and others. Memories of the war are back with a vengeance, and nobody trusts anybody anymore. There are tales of mass graves, songs of collective hysteria. Words open wounds. Everyone is smarting.

It was the Slovenes who conjured up the demons of the Serb-Croat conflict, but it was the Yugoslav Army's brutal entry into Kosovo in the interest of "Greater Serbia" (and against the interest of the local Albanian population) that hastened the Slovenes' withdrawal from the Republic. Croatia's Serbs fear being turned from a privileged to an underprivileged minority and say they would rather die. But the aspirations of the Serbs as a nation clash with reality: they are demanding things that are not theirs or only partly theirs. If all Serbs are to live in a nation-state, they must rule over large minorities of other nations. If a nation wants something that does not belong to it, reality will eventually teach it a painful lesson.

The Slovenes defend themselves well, but I cannot entirely sympathize with their cause either. Does a rich man abandon his poor relatives with a simple "We have nothing in common"? Has Slovenia in fact so little in common with the rest of the country? It did choose Yugoslavia twice, after all. Does it think it will place all its wares in the West? The Slovenes are eager to join the rich, but the rich are not particularly eager to have them. When Slovenes tell West Europeans, "We are leaving Yugoslavia for the Common Market," they get wry smiles in return, and only European civility keeps the smiles from being put into words: "You are leaving a hornet's nest behind you. *Après vous le déluge.*"

What about Croatia? It is demanding an oath of allegiance from its minority Serbs, a ritual of duplicity and self-denial. What are the criteria for allegiance? And what will happen to those who refuse to take the oath? Will they be deported, expatriated?

Identities are necessarily partial, hence self-contradictory; moreover by their very nature they are exclusionary. The more you set your mind to a thing, the more militantly you go about it. For every case of embattled autonomy or imaginary identity there is a "just cause" and spoils to be divided.

Politicians love to take a word and make it their own. Identity lures you into a nightclub that then fleeces you. "Joining Europe" is now all the rage. If you haven't applied, you're out in the cold. Identity is a spiritual prosthesis for those of middling intelligence, a ready-made text implanted in the brain.

Politicians, priests, journalists, and intellectual careerists would herd us into corrals. Whose stall do you choose? Tracts on identity are chiefly yellow-press claptrap. What gives leaders power are their texts for the man in the street about where his loyalty lies. The sooner you swallow the identity bait, the sooner you are in the politicians' hands.

I categorize them according to how dangerous they are. Why do we define ourselves in so few words? I am a member of that unfortunate race known as human whose curse is imperfect knowledge. What are you? Albanian? Serb? Volunteer soldier? Fine. Feel like a little sniping? Sometimes a body feels like a little sniping. Find a tank and off you go.

Beer-bellied paterfamilias types are now big bullies. When they come around with their machine guns asking for your ID, you show it to them, you let them search your briefcase and your car. They have instant authorization.

The past is back. Young men are playing war again. They haven't begun to feel the suffering yet: death by the hundred thousand is ancient history on both sides. Grandson has taken up where grandfather left off: village against village. They've all seen no end of partisan films.

Now that the Soviet Army is gone, local units feel the need to flex their armored limbs. The armed patriots are attracted as much by the grim camouflage of battle dress as by operetta uniforms.

While a pacifist scholar of Buddhism was aiming his camera at a tank rattling down the street below his hotel balcony, the tank's gun aimed back and mowed him down. Every young man shot is a murder. When callow youths are given guns and uniforms and instructed to go out head-hunting, it makes no difference what nation they belong to. The text that authorizes anyone to shoot anyone is an evil text.

Yugoslavia has no tyrant. There is no one to kill. Nobody's death will solve anything. Anyone with any sense will hand back his weapon with the words, "There's no one for me to shoot." Anyone who fails to do so is politically brain-damaged. "Come to your senses!" I want to tell them all. "Don't shout, 'Serbia or death! Slovenia or death!' There's no point in either killing or dying for one or the other." Anyone who considers another nation—the sons of another nation—his mortal enemy is drunk on words. Any grown-up Yugoslav who reaches for a gun instead of a compromise is mentally a child and does not deserve national sovereignty because he lacks personal sovereignty—the ability to control himself.

Wherever people fight and kill, everyone is wrong. No side is pure; all sides go too far. Each side exaggerates its identity and the consequences thereof; each side believes that its national character takes precedence over its mortal character. Wherever people fight and kill, thinkers have not been doing their duty—or, rather, they have been doing it badly, failing to meet their responsibility and prepare both sides for a dialogue that leads to a compromise. Though it is far from easy to find a compromise between raging parties whose shared rhetoric goads them on to greater rage.

When the nationality conflict obliterates all else and the high priests of the intelligentsia support their nation's obsession with romantic platitudes, we have what can be called political hysteria. A change in regime is especially propitious for national identity searches because people are no longer saying what they said yesterday and need to learn who they really are, to gain a firm, incontestable picture of themselves, one that has stood and will continue to stand the test of time, a superior picture, something they can pledge their loyalty to, serve, obey like good children. And so we have Mother Tongue and Fatherland. The real issue is not so much whether we love our roots— loving the place where we were born, like loving our parents, is only natural and needs no special injunction—as whether we identify with our mother tongue and the earth that nurtured it or with our fatherland and the state power that oversees its borders.

Hysteria also comes from others' doubting that we are what we say we are or preventing us from being what we say we are. It is closely related to the sullen resentment fashionable in Eastern Europe whenever the issue of national identity comes up, though it is an issue we cannot afford to sweep under the rug. What must have once appeared to the Western observer an ethnological peculiarity has now assumed the proportions of a personality disorder.

The English aren't hysterical. They don't go on about being English; they don't need to. The very idea of making an issue of "Englishness" (the word doesn't exist) they find distasteful, though no one can deny them an emotional attachment to tradition. "But I'm not English!" the petulant East European objects. "You can say that again," I reply.

Hysteria allows the idea of national identity to take on racial dimensions. Suddenly there are superior and inferior races, useful and harmful races, races to be cultivated and races to be exterminated. Suddenly human solidarity can be denied some races for ideological reasons.

How politicians deal with these issues, which often boil down to matters of prestige, is one thing; how seriously we ordinary people ought to take them is something else. It is only natural that fascist-oriented politicians should dislike being lumped together with humanity as a whole: their cause thrives on the specific.

By now we have been privy to a number of heated divorce proceedings. No person is more despicable than the person you have most recently shared your bed with, no nation more wicked than the nation you have most recently shared your state with. You wake up one morning to find you can't live with them anymore.

While Western Europe moves towards multicultural integration, Eastern Europe moves towards monocultural disintegration. We have postnationalism in the West, prenationalism in the East. Must things fall asunder before they can come together? And what of the people with a multiracial makeup and multicultural lives? In the end, we all have multiple identities. By privileging one, we stifle the others.

We set limits to our broadmindedness: this far and no farther. It may take some gnashing of teeth, but we do love Europeans (read: the peoples *we* define as Europeans). We feel no obligation whatever to "non-Europeans" and refuse to share with them: they have nothing in common with us.

Building Europe means building a rational legal system on the basis of commonly held legal principles; it means creative intervention in the legal system of individual states; it means compatible constitutions. The politician's true duty is to make laws (and the public opinion to go with them) that keep people from killing one another.

Eastern Europe needs to import democratic decision-making formulas. Can western rationalism work in the highly confused conditions of Eastern Europe? Can Europe's eastern half espouse

Western spiritual as well as material concerns, what we might call the European and American variety of humanism?

More mature politicians must take less mature colleagues under their wing. The West must defuse the language of tribal animosity. Now that the East can no longer form international alliances against the West, tribalism has little chance of holding out for long: the anti-imperialist, socialist bloc was the bloc of the backward, the bloc of resentment, and the bond uniting antiwestern nationalisms disappeared with the passing of socialism.

Which is more likely, the Europeanization of the Balkans or the Balkanization of Europe? The South Slavs no longer find it enough to be Yugoslavs—or, rather, they find it too much. What should Europe offer them instead? Civil war is not the best visiting card to present to the European Community. Nor do the parties involved wish to set up a Central European Confederation. They are aspiring to something more prestigious: to be the first to get a foot in the Europa-Club door.

The Austro-Hungarian Compromise of 1877 was wise in that it reconciled opposing interests. Naturally an agreement of the sort does not completely satisfy each party, the whole idea of compromise implying limited satisfaction, an accommodation with reality, with others, an alliance for common causes. Yet it is an approach that might be applied with profit to the conflict in Yugoslavia today.

We must also recognize the viability of the heterogeneous nation-state. Most states are heterogeneous: Great Britain, France, Italy, Spain, Germany . . . In them a number of relatively independent entities, identities, agree to live together under a single jurisdiction and a single set of laws.

Before the First World War Hungary was a heterogeneous

nation-state. The trouble was that its elite refused to think through the consequences of heterogeneity. If a nation harbors sizable minorities within its pale and has no long-range plan for minority autonomy, it feeds a hysteria that can only end badly.

The "eastern" way of thinking is again joining church and state and using a hysterical national rhetoric to do so. Proponents of national homogenization are showing less and less tolerance for the multinational, multicultural nation-state. The West is confused: it couldn't take the East back into the fold until Communism fell, but now that Communism has fallen, it can't take it back because a xenophobic hornet's nest is in the making.

Western Europe's fascination with the East won't last forever. Even now people are saying that we're a bunch of primitive, squabbling hatemongers who use our new-found freedom of speech to call our neighbors names, that we either beg for charity or ask exorbitant prices for shoddy goods and services and then take umbrage when our Western partners point out where we have failed or misbehaved.

Are they right?

1991

Dematerializing Borders

The word *fascism* having become criminalized, we cannot easily apply it to current events: by invoking it, we invoke the specter of mass murder. We might say *national fundamentalism* and *national radicalism,* distinguishing them by their compatibility with parliamentary democracy. In the interest of linguistic and conceptual clarity, however, we shall use the term *neofascism.* Neofascism has naturally adapted to the changes that have occurred over the last half-century, but its rhetoric stems from the same line of thought.

Eastern Europe is a region where Catholicism, Protestantism, Orthodoxy, and Islam meet, a region that gives rise to new national identities. These identities are very real. The Soviet Empire suppressed them, but shared feelings will eventually out. The belief that the experience of a common history can be buried has proved to be an illusion. No insult can be undone; collectives remember, and the pain of former offenses and humiliations grows.

The minority issue was starting to subside in the region until three changes took place.

1. The democratic movement that brought about the more or less radical reforms of 1989 (which were actually a compromise between the ruling party elite and a technocracy that had fallen under opposition influence) raised minority consciousness and encouraged the formation of minority organizations.

2. National dissension arose not only among majority and minority nations but also among nations in federative states such as Czechoslovakia and Yugoslavia. Thus the states created after the First World War were suddenly in crisis. Both north and south of Hungary powerful Slav nations—Czechs, Serbs— had formed federations with one or more other Slav nations. But now nations with mutually comprehensible languages are calling for autonomy and even separatism. If two nations' right to statehood is recognized as valid, why shouldn't other countries break up into nations of their own?

3. Now that the Soviet Empire has ceased to be monolithic, problems among its nationalities are making themselves felt. We are sitting on a powder keg of internationality relations, yet to be established, in a new state that is projecting its own struggles across the whole of Europe.

Western Europe, Catholic and Protestant, is withdrawing from Orthodox Europe. Many feel that Orthodox Europe is not yet ready for political rationalism, that it seeks to sanctify trans-individual concepts, that it is paternalistic, in other words, unhappy until it can find a father figure. None of this is foreign to Central and Southwest Europe either, of course. At the very least, however, ethnic conflicts in the former Soviet region give a new dimension to the nationality issue.

National ideas and movements are a means of superimposing a homogeneous, postfeudal structure upon a nation that a minority has joined rather than been born to. Members of the outsider minority must pledge ethnic and national loyalty in addition to civic loyalty; they must agree to fuse with the nation. And what better way to spur fusion than by coercion?

If the minority refuses to give up its identity, the emotional pendulum swings in the other direction: love us or leave us. The majority calls for dissimilation—keep your distance, we refuse to have anything to do with you, we don't want you polluting our blood—and comes up with a theory to prove its superiority. We might even say that the point at which things shade into fascism is when the majority starts giving pseudohistorical, pseudoscientific, race-based proof of the recalcitrant minority's inferiority. There are such things as spontaneous aversions; they are part of the nature of things and unorganized. But fascistoid movements use ideology to transform individual aversions into an all-encompassing, theoretically justified collective hate.

Large empires channel their hatreds. They assume hatred exists and must be guided productively, aimed logically and consistently. But now a new situation has arisen. Stray hatreds have taken over the great central ones, regional, local, neighborhood hatreds, wandering about wherever the population is ethnically mixed and the majority nation is thinking of digesting or, on the contrary, spitting out its minorities (as the Poles did with the Jews in 1969 or the Bulgarians with the Turks in the eighties). Dissimilation by state mandate. To the chance, far-removed television viewer this internecine squabbling must seem more than alien; it must seem insane, a rerun of the African tribal wars, which the world endorses. "If they're so intent on gobbling one another up, let them," says the jaded viewer, switching to another channel.

Several ideas for dealing with the situation have come forward. The superpowers, for example, might take the responsibility for establishing order and promulgate a European Magna Carta. But what can we do for ourselves?

For one thing, we can introduce dual citizenship. A person with two citizenships is protected by two states. Collecting citizenships might even turn into a hobby. One passport affords a sense of self, two passports—a double sense of self. Denying the right to dual citizenship is denying a basic human right. If a Hungarian living in Australia has the right to a Hungarian passport, why should a Hungarian living in Romania or Slovakia be denied one?

Dual or multiple loyalty is perfectly natural. Nothing is more typical of our culture than people living on the fault line of a painful conflict, the result, say, of a mixed marriage. When large numbers of people hold each other's citizenship, when countries award honorary citizenship to large numbers of foreigners, common interest groups are bound to spring up across borders.

Another possibility is to rethink the very concept of the border. Borders are not sacred; indeed, the best border is an inconspicuous one. We need to dematerialize the border, reduce its power to carry on operations and impede the flow of traffic. As the border erodes, people who belong together will come together.

An express train can run from Budapest halfway across Romania to Marosvásárhely in three hours. If there is going to be an unmonitored connection between the West Bank and Gaza and there was an unmonitored connection between West Germany and West Berlin, why can't there be one between Hungary and Romania?

We are living in a society that is increasingly on the move. Political systems can no longer be based on impregnable borders. Dual citizenship and cross-boundary mobility are ideas whose time has suddenly come.

1991

What Is the Charter?

It is a mental and spiritual coalition of democrats. It is not a party, only a network of like-minded people. It has no members, only signers. It is a public handshake between the people who happened to compile it and the people who happen to sign it. It is not so much an organization as an ongoing exchange of ideas. It is a made-in-Hungary citizens' initiative, though it has no borders and may eventually give rise to analogous experiments among neighbors or even farther afield: Latin America and Southeast Asia—and perhaps even the European Union —could use democratic charters of their own. And by putting "democratic charter" in the plural, I am implying that no one has a monopoly on it. In fact, I see it more as a genre than a fixed text.

A civil society continually makes its expectations known to its government and to public opinion in general. The Charter will continue to exist only if thinking people continue to agree with it at each step of the way.

A civil society proceeds by trial and error towards forms appropriate to making its expectations known. The Charter has no desire to supplant representative democracy. It wishes to help establish an elected government and (in the long run) a political class in a democratic environment. It wishes to serve as a third party in two-party conflicts—between ethnic or national groups, for instance. It wishes to become a free, transnational, interpersonal association that keeps the philosophy of democracy fresh and alive, disseminating it everywhere freedom-loving people gather to exchange ideas.

The Charter can be a spokesmanlike body for making various viewpoints on issues of public interest known, though such a function should not gain the upper hand. We are starting something completely new, and I personally would feel uncomfortable with the idea of any impersonal, institutional supervision. If there are objections to any text, I am perfectly willing to rework it.

The Charter provides a more personal form of feedback than the public opinion poll. My signature makes me more than a number: it makes me a name and everything my fellow citizens know about me; it means I take a stand in favor of or against something, I give my civic approval or disapproval to something that pleases or offends my democratic sensibility. I don't take a four-year Sleeping Beauty rest between elections.

I realize my political representatives have a great deal to do in Parliament and on the local level, but I don't feel politics stops there. Politics—that is, the debate of issues concerning us all—must not become a distant buzz from above.

It is good for people to gather periodically and have their say. It is good for representatives and nonrepresentatives, elected officials and electors to take part in well-run public discussions as equals. It is good to arrive at formulations in groups, because a group tempers the follies of individuals.

A text thus engendered has a certain discipline about it, a democratic self-restraint. It may not be poetic or philosophical, but it does represent a consensus. When people sit together in a room, they can debate every adjective, vote on every verb. A text does not try to make friends of enemies; it merely asks its readers whether they agree with its theses.

The Democratic Charter vindicates a certain style. There are things a group of people who respect one another cannot bring itself to do. It will not, for instance, indulge in the kind of deceitful mudslinging that pollutes the linguistic environment.

If the government interprets signing the Charter as a gesture of disloyalty, we must ask it to define what it means by government service and what sort of loyalty it requires of its various categories of employees (given that most of the population, even now, is employed by the state). Are we to understand that, as in the Kádár period, state employees are forbidden to sign? Or is it only those in high positions, at the ministerial level? What about policemen, teachers, judges, managers? Or people applying for state grants? Must the theater where the Charter was first formulated close its doors to Charter meetings? Will it be in danger of losing its government subsidy if it is identified with the Charter?

The Democratic Charter is necessary because the rhetoric of punishment is constantly on the lookout for a target and scapegoat for public unrest. The Charter is a spiritual shield against those who would punish opposition. Yet since—we repeat—it is not a party, has no membership, and represents no more than agreement in principle on a case-by-case basis, it invests power in none. It is not our power, it is our influence.

By thinking together in this way, we also wish to ensure that the new democracies of the nineties will follow the Western, civil pattern rather than the Eastern, feudal one with its arrogance of power and humiliating hierarchical allegiances. Because most of the population in our country and in this part of the world still holds state or state-controlled jobs, the temptation to return to a state-socialist, state-controlled system is great. Communism carried out a major purge among the elite of the Horthy regime, but it retained and even intensified the regime's feudal, administrative control. The closer we observe the current regime's ruling style, the more we wonder whether *its* purge is not merely a rhetorical smoke screen covering what amounts to structural continuity.

What matters more than which people are assigned to refute critical commentary in the press and which abstract nouns they use to do so is the fact of the refutation itself. A clever government learns from the criticism aimed at it.

A multiparty system and a democratic constitution will not automatically guarantee the formation of a democratic society. We must look upon the transition to democracy as a learning process of indefinite duration, unthinkable without a many-sided, many-headed, many-faced public. The heavy-handed state apparatus we have inherited can still be used against us. If we regressed into a dictatorship, we would not be able to meet in this room. Hungary is in the process of becoming a democracy, but we don't yet know how that process will end.

It is important that no one be allowed to put a personal stamp on our country, our parties, our cities and towns. It is important that through all its four years in power the coalition enjoying the majority in Parliament be confronted with fresh versions of the basic democratic values, values that it too benefits from, after all. The Democratic Charter represents a rejuvenation of the idea of the social contract on the part of the governed.

By virtue of that idea the Charter is open to all. Anyone may sign, that is, anyone who has thought its message through and is in agreement with it. Signing without agreeing will not make anyone sleep easier, however, because signing does not entitle anyone to anything or count in anyone's favor. Or against anyone, for that matter.

The Democratic Charter may grow and multiply; it may even multiply by fission. It is not surrounded by a fence jealously protecting its articles of faith. In all probability it will give rise to mindless imitations, but there is one way of proving that a text is genuinely Charter-related: the thought it expresses. In a kind of immune reaction the democratic thought process rejects all restrictions on freedom and any justification of same.

The arrogance of power wounded is an argument against itself. Mudslinging is self-accusation. Antidemocratic ideas cannot be merchandised in the name of the Democratic Charter. Its trademark consists of its name, its signatures, and the people willing to identify themselves with it.

The current government would not be wise to reject the Charter out of hand: it may have need of it once it is out of power. Nor should the opposition parties think of it as a harmless toy: they too can be burned. In other words, the Charter is not to be taken lightly. By signing it, you agree to abide by its rules, and you will have it on your conscience if you do not.

We, the governed, must keep reminding them, the government, of the conditions of the social contract. We pay taxes for our peace of mind, and we expect our government officials to bring the necessary equilibrium and expertise to their tasks. If they fail—fail to provide us with electricity, say—then we can look elsewhere. As citizens we pay taxes, not tribute, and we must make it perfectly clear what we pay them for.

The Democratic Charter is not a new discovery; it developed out of the arsenal of our democratic movement as what I have called a "genre" for organizing public opinion in a civil society. This is a difficult task, one that emphasizes the interpersonal. The Charter's participants thus sign as individuals rather than legal entities. If that raises a few eyebrows and people say, "Oh, a parlor game," I don't mind. I'd rather see our public life a playing field than a battlefield. The best way to respond to the Charter's seventeen points—which are by no means perfect—is to replace them with seventeen better points.

It is possible, as I have said, that similarly inclined democrats in other countries will form their own democratic charters, and there is nothing more natural than that they should come together in a supranational network, nothing more natural than that such a transnational moral authority should serve to temper national conflicts and defend beleaguered minorities. In disputes between neighbors a third-party arbiter often proves beneficial.

Countries and parties have a harder time coming to an agreement than individuals. A Hungary and a Europe of individuals may be able to play a more valuable and up-to-date role than a Hungary and Europe of institutions. Be it therefore resolved: Everyone who signs the Democratic Charter shall be considered its honorary spokesperson. I also envisage a small board of spokespersons, a group whose membership changes on a yearly basis.

What you clench in your fist may seep through your fingers.

Our experiment may come to nought. But even if it does, it will return in a different form. One of the reasons I find it so attractive in its present form is that it can't be pinned down. We don't quite know what it is, this concerted nod in the direction of a few basic related principles. It may take flight, it may fall on its face, but the spirit of civic pride will keep the idea alive and try out ever new variations.

Experience shows that personal freedom is not easily violated as long as we ourselves refuse to contribute to its violation, refuse to give it up.

1991

Being a Citizen

(Words of Encouragement to Signers of the Democratic Charter, Budapest, 19 December 1991)

Democratic Ladies and Gentlemen!

You have nothing to fear.

If normal citizens behave in a normal, civic manner and assume others around them will do the same; if they have the self-confidence that comes of knowing how to do something well, of doing a good job at work, and of being able to handle several chess games at once; if they don't expect life to be handed to them on a silver platter in exchange for lifelong obedience; if they can go it alone, do not curry favor, and are consequently capable of natural, long-term friendships; if they are not worn down by everyday iniquities; if they can brush off insults with a shrug of the shoulders or even a laugh—because what they really care about is playing, talking, working, doing business, arguing, coming to agreements, fighting, helping, and loving as decently as possible—then you, as citizens, have nothing to fear.

When we say "decently," we mean warmly and openly; we

mean a give and take of information, a readiness to engage in dialogue, to stand up for one's opinions on humanity or politics without condemning rationally based counteropinions as erroneous, condemning only the condemnation of counteropinions as erroneous, condemning the transformation of political differences into disparagement or even grounds for removal from the playing field—behavior that might be called unsportsmanlike, though I would use terms a good deal harsher.

Citizens in our sense of the word can be hot or cold according to the situation, but they are always ashamed to be rude, to lie, cheat, or steal, to envy or betray, let alone kill, the cardinal sin. Citizens in our sense of the word refrain from making judgments; they follow the ethical strategy set forth by László Németh in his essay on Tolstoy: they are hard on themselves and easy on others.

Citizens have nothing to fear if they recognize that what counts is what they do themselves and that what others do neither accuses them of nor excuses them from anything. By acting accordingly, they will get on reasonably well with others, especially if they do not expect too much. What they should expect is the absence of the threat of violence by the state or the individual, this being one of civilization's basic minimums, and they will thus accept nothing less than that they should live in a state ruled by law.

Why shouldn't any thinking civilian or similarly inclined soldier, priest, or politician (in silence, in a moment of discretion, having put their non-civic roles in parentheses) ascribe to the extraordinarily simple concept set forth in the founding charter of the now seventy-year-old International PEN Club, namely, that all members shall work with whatever means they have at their disposal to further understanding among human beings without regard to race, nation, nationality, class, or religion and defend the freedom to express their own opinions in the face of any and all forms of censorship?

That this perfectly simple principle enables writers from every part of the world to agree on all manner of questions concerning the freedom and solidarity of those who live by the pen proves that the PEN Club charter is more effective than any ideology or religion: unlike them it has been able to create unanimity around the globe and harmony across cultures. Why shouldn't the position articulated in the PEN charter be the position not exclusively of the poets, essayists, and novelists who sign it but of any literate citizen?

Two basic values, autonomy and solidarity, serve as helpful prompters in any decision-making process. They are like siblings who sometimes play together and sometimes fight; they coexist in all sorts of situations and in the choices we make every day. If we are in touch with what is going on inside us, we are less likely to consider one or the other entirely in the right. The best we can do is hitch them both to a wagon whose driver we may have some inkling of but whose passenger we do not know at all.

As a citizen I do anything I approve of and nothing I disapprove of. I try not to talk myself into the dirty tricks others might do in my place.

Citizens have nothing to fear if they keep their word. As our forefathers put it: One man, one word. People who speak falsely or lightly, who say first one thing, then another—whatever happens to be current—have no credibility and might well ask themselves what they do have.

Citizens jealous of their honor always make the best of what they have. They do not palm off shoddy goods. They regard bad service as tantamount to robbery. They do not beg. They are always ready to give someone a leg up, but don't complain about not getting one in return.

Every morning they give thanks to their Creator or Fate for keeping them alive, for letting them kick off the covers, for giving them breakfast. And if they have reason to believe they are being stalked by death, they bless what may be their last day on earth.

Citizens are fallible, and their religion and philosophy are the religion and philosophy of the weak. Everything they have they are likely to abuse. Because we know and understand this (that is, because we have observed it in others and in ourselves), we must strengthen our hands by playing the game according to mutually accepted rules instead of trying to beat the system. Beating the system makes no sense in a democracy.

Democracy means sensible realism, a legal order based on an awareness of man's inclination to abuse it, a legal order with checks and balances. It means that everyone has a right to voice an opinion, but implies respect for sound arguments and impatience with hot air. It means preferring clarity of thought to the rhetoric of emotion. Calling what lurks behind the latter "mischief" is very much an understatement.

Thus the civic element represents a taste, a style, a pattern of behavior that promotes the innate equality of every human being in every way possible. And while it does not in the least oppose such natural parent/child, teacher/pupil, doctor/patient authority relationships, it would free them from disdain and overweening self-importance, from the "It's so because I say so" argument, from flattery, an anxious desire to please, an unconditional willingness to do the master's bidding—in short, from everything that must be reappraised if both nobleman and serf are to become citizens, if class pride is to give way to a sense of self-pride and servility to civility.

Citizens know that a tool reflects its user, that the theory and practice of political purges is a boomerang that will hit the hard-nosed perpetrator the hardest. They are able to separate sympathy and antipathy from legality. They do not confuse faith and craft, that is, they do not use political or religious arguments in professional matters, and they consider their colleagues' political or religious views as private as their sexual preferences.

Citizens feel gratified if they can dip into their surplus to provide for the less fortunate. They help their fellow citizens as they can—volunteering, applying a fresh coat of paint, giving gifts.

Citizens who are in it for the long haul have no reason to fear: in time the good-for-nothings may turn out to have been merely not so good, and they can always be voted out. In any case, we've made it through another year. What the new year will bring remains to be seen. If we want it to bring something better, we need to regroup and do a bit more stretching.

The Holiday Looks Back

(A Speech Made in Petőfi Square on 15 March 1992
Celebrating the Democratic Charter)

Signers of the Democratic Charter! Ladies and Gentlemen!

Here we are together in Petőfi Square in the presence of
the poet and his friends, the perfect context to evoke the mythology of freedom: the greatest Hungarian holiday, a festive
occasion we never tire of. If there is a national holiday we can
celebrate year in and year out with renewed passion, it is the
fifteenth of March.

What the poets, law students, and journeymen—stimulated
by events and improvising their own playful yet visionary
scenario—accomplished on that day in 1848 has been neither
invalidated nor even tarnished in the intervening century and
a half.

There have been times when the day was commemorated
with hypocrisy, times when the statue of Petőfi (which, though
not particularly accomplished, is dear to our hearts) was surrounded by policemen and police dogs, times when it called
forth swords and truncheons, times when it was plastered with

muddled manifestos. But the monument protests, the holiday looks back. The eyes of the ides of March pierce the garrulous gloom.

On the fifteenth of March the city dared to play! It played out its desires, and the play turned out to be revolution. Everything worked together on that day. Even the rain conspired to raise people's spirits: huddled under umbrellas, heedless of the drops trickling down their collars, they hung on the speakers' every word.

Everything was well thought out and well executed: the parallels to events throughout Europe, the list of points drawn up in the nearby Pilvax Café, the procession to the University, the market, the Museum, and on to the printer's, where Landerer, the master printer, counseled the gentlemen to seize the press. It was this glorious laying on of hands by the poet in the name of the people—the public lifting of a ban—that proved the high point of the revolution. Then the liberation of Táncsics, the messages, the pronouncements, and finally the gala performance in the National Theater—they were all early, totally unprecedented manifestations of the revolution's poetic ritual order in this city. On 23 October 1956 I could not help feeling how much of what happened was marked by its 15 March 1848 prototype.

The fifteenth of March is the day of the Hungarian avantgarde. The young people did not mince their words. They spoke in the name of their fellow citizens but said what they themselves thought. In their eyes freedom for Hungary and world freedom were twin concepts.

At the moment when idea and opportunity came together, the young writers accomplished something irreversible: they

created an atmosphere that made any curtailment of the freedom of the press, any accommodation with the censors a matter
of embarrassment. No one can want any less than what they
wanted.

The day that destroyed censorship and separated truth from
falsehood is the day when the moral level of the Hungarian
intellectual can first be measured. Petőfi has been present in us
from the start, and we recognize flashes of his wisdom in our
finest hours.

The Diet and therefore the politicians were in Pressburg at
the time. The fifteenth of March was the doing of nonprofes-
sionals. On 15 March the layman entered history.

Petőfi and his followers did not want power, they wanted
freedom, constitutionally guaranteed freedom, and to get it they
formed a powerful opposition. No one appointed them to the
role; they were empowered to seize it by their genius. No one
asked them what right they had to speak; they were heard
because they had something to say.

As I see it, the spirit of 1848 is not at all alien to our
initiative in favor of a civic society, to our seventeen points,
our Democratic Charter. The seventeen points are basically a
civic initiative. What is the purpose of the Democratic Charter
a century and a half after Petőfi and shortly after our constitutional revolution? Why have we, who feel at one with the
seventeen points and the mode of thought they represent—
why have we come together? To celebrate and to revel in our
numbers.

By signing the Charter, we have stood up for certain basic
democratic principles. Signing the Charter is not like voting
by secret ballot; it is a public gesture, a call for dialogue. The

seventeen points are seventeen discussion topics, a table of contents for the main issue: Do we want genuine democracy or are we satisfied with window dressing?

Now that everybody and his uncle call themselves democrats, what gives us our identity? What is our national platform? How do we picture the relationship between the individual and the state? How may we order our relationships with one another so as to live free and secure lives? How may we ensure that a citizen need not fear the state or feel at its mercy?

A constitution does not come alive until its principles and practice are confronted on a daily basis. To prevent conflict from escalating, we favor the resumption of nationwide round-table discussions based on just such a living constitution. Otherwise the level of argumentation may sink so low that the participants will start shooting at one another. The history of Central Europe thunders with degenerate argumentation.

The Democratic Charter means reformulating—that is, keeping alive—the democratic process and our common values. The example is spreading. Colleagues in other countries are thinking of drawing up democratic charters commensurate with their own concerns and mentalities. Recently a Latvian journalist gave me a copy of the Latvian Democratic Charter. Given the transition problems our entire region is facing, it would not be amiss to have a democratic charter for East-Central Europe. Europe's eastern half needs a common authority at least until it joins the European Union. We need a democratic charter as a gauge, a means of telling sham democracy from the real thing.

Nowadays even autocracies want to appear democratic, but all they really care about is packaging their beliefs in such a way as to keep them intact. The Charter's platform actively encourages the signers to develop it by engaging other intelligent people in dialogue. People involved in the debate must continue to hear what others are saying; they must not prejudge the truth according to political affiliation. We will be successful only if the game does not degenerate into a free-for-all.

What lies at the heart of the Charter? The survival of humanity. Government by law. Respect for individuals and minorities. Freedom of thought. Moderation of state power. Now that everyone has a right to speak, you are responsible if you speak and responsible if you do not.

Democratic charters are particularly needed in the countries of Eastern Europe to counterbalance the state's tendency to absolute power. Since our societies, economies, and cultures have depended predominantly on the state, government has traditionally had access to the citizens' heads. Now *a* party has replaced *the* party, yet the redistribution of wealth and power remains centralized, and this at a time when the country's fiscal burden, as we all know, is far from negligible. Moreover, the state's sense of social responsibility appears to be waning faster than its authority to intervene. A government that roundly condemns socialism still has the tools of the socialist state and its monitoring bodies at its command. It can therefore vilify the previous system and pillory its officials while continuing to carry on its practices.

Given that the new regulations will for a time reduce buying power and consequently increase the population's feeling of defenselessness, many hesitate to sign the Charter for fear of losing their jobs. Yet when teachers and journalists must again watch their tongues, when the finely tuned reflexes of self-censorship are back at work, when people once more feel their well-being depends on the government, when the state is over-weight and shows no signs of going on a diet, the Democratic

Charter is a necessity. Not until democratic self-control is on a par with governmental authority and members of the ruling party stop using obvious tricks and the taxpayers' money to curb untrammeled public opinion will the need for the Charter diminish.

In our situation everyone is a beginner. Even the elderly are trying their luck. But who finances our leaders' mistakes? The taxpayers. Some with their lives, their goods and chattels, others with anxiety and straitened circumstances. The change in regime has done away with the people who claimed responsibility for the country. In a democratic parliament an election defeat can unseat a government. The electorate may suddenly feel there is no one in charge, but to rely on a government merely because it is in charge is the height of imprudence: society pays the bill in the end.

The possibility of slipping back into an authoritarian regime—anti-socialist but with all the accoutrements of state socialism—is not out of the question. Many people are concerned about where the country is heading, but none of them seem to be politicians—or wish to be. Meanwhile, the government is doing its best to transform an independent press into a totally dependent one. Surely the public needs to raise a collective eyebrow.

A raised eyebrow would be especially justified on this day when we celebrate the freedom of the press and when at another public meeting, organized by the ruling party in front of the radio and television building, reporters and newscasters are being threatened to toe the line. Why is it only the opposition press that rates the government's uncommonly acrid commentary? Why not the extreme right? Do our leaders consider liberal criticism more galling than ultra-conservative? I don't know which I find more unfortunate: that such is their taste or that such is their tactics.

We who have signed the Charter must confront the constitutional principle of freedom of the press with this clear-cut attempt to intimidate the media. We can have democracy only if we do not have intimidation. In European democracies the government holds freedom of press and the decisions of the constitutional court in high regard. Every attempt to circumvent the logic of the law by means of subterfuge comes to light and miscarries.

We can pretend to be democrats, but we will fool neither the country nor the world any more than children who believe they are hiding when they cover their eyes with their hands. Like it or not, Hungary—together with Central Europe as a whole—is fated to be a democracy. And as the Latin proverb has it, fate leads the willing and drags the reluctant.

15 March: A Colorful Day

On 14 March we drove to Budapest from the country. The boys fell asleep in the car. I had written my 15 March speech last week—moaning and groaning or, rather, cursing, as if it were homework—because writing for a crowd is different from writing for a lone reader. I picture a reader similar to me. But a crowd? Who knows?

I worked in my basement office, cutting the text. Then I printed it up and showed it to Jutka, who said, "Too long." Nothing more. In other words, no good. "It's impossible to say anything original in a square, at a mass meeting," she added by way of sympathy.

By three in the morning I'd condensed it even more. I decided to concentrate on freedom of the press, because the government wanted to be the sole voice and was out to get the TV, radio, and newspapers. Rumor had it that a band of ruffians would put in an appearance.

Far-right organizations calling for "genuine Hungarian and

Christian media" (which translates into "Kick the Jews out of the press") did in fact show up. The people doing the shouting were woebegone, crumpled types, their faces flushed with alcohol. They cursed, they fumed, but what bothered them most was that they hadn't received compensation for their years in prison. Although the opposition liberals, the Free Democrats, were the first to propose that former political prisoners be compensated, these people believe the liberals are to blame for their being ignored: the liberals refuse to slap prison terms on the Communists, don't they? Somewhere or other they have branded me a "liberal Bolshevik."

It was drizzling. By half past ten the hecklers had filed past the Petőfi statue and disappeared. All at once the sun came out. Some friends waved happily. I lifted my head to the rays breaking through the clouds and read out what I'd written. It was well received. The square was full. The Democratic Charter had the best attended rally in Budapest.

There was no cause for concern in our square: no one was playing on emotions, and no one made a hero of people who refuse to listen to reason. *Our* square wants to abide by the rules of the game and talk things through—with humor if possible. *Their* square was all fuss and bluster, resentment and sulking; it was a square of blunt speech.

In Petőfi Square about fifteen thousand people applauded me; two hours later in Freedom Square about a hundred people wanted to beat me up. A lot of people like me, but there are some who hate me. An odd day. Sometimes a single mad hater is enough.

They formed a U around me. "Tell us why you hate us, Mr. Konrád, why you hate us Hungarians." "I'm afraid of you, Mr. Konrád. I get this physical feeling of fear when I look at you. I start to tremble." "Long live György Konrád, the greatest Hungarian writer! But not too long!" A rather decent-looking gentleman stepped forward and shouted, "Traitor!" but when I said to his face, "How can you say such a thing?" he backed off. They're free with their insults in a pack, but one-on-one they back off.

Jutka: "You're as much of an ass as your son when he insisted he wanted a gun at the age of two. Why go? Why provoke them? Why make them more important than they are? Don't you realize what they stand for, those neofascists?"

The filmmaker Károly Makk and I started off for the car at a purposefully dignified pace. A pair of motorcycle policemen sensed danger in the air and made themselves scarce. Paying them no heed, we sauntered on in the direction of the car and got in. The crowd surrounded it from the front end, and some skinheads started pounding the body. Because our way was blocked in front, Károly shifted into reverse, and as we shot backward there were a few kisses blown and a few fists shaken.

Next day, looking back at the events from the privacy of my country cottage, I saw myself as a silent-film character. It's no big deal, you don't need to be swept up in it, you can always walk away if the rhetoric gets to you. The older people are, the more they like to talk, the more they fight for the mike. My urgent sense of responsibility is a trap. I should learn to fend off the moral challenges of public life with a joke. I'm glad to be alive, glad to be where I am. I don't know what's in store for me, but I'm curious about the next episode.

Most men have a hunter in them, and a hunter can always kill another man. I am not a hunter—I'm on the other side: the prey. I know what it's like when hunters and hounds surround you. You turn and smile, though sooner or later they're bound to pounce.

Even though my circle of friends is wider than my circle of enemies, I find it strange that there should be people in Budapest whom I infuriate merely by standing next to them with my mouth shut, not saying a word, not bothering them in the slightest, just standing there.

They came to kick up a row and take over the TV. They assumed the government would let them do it: they have a common enemy, after all—the press. But in the end they found themselves up against a wall of policemen, and when they turned away incensed, what did they see?

Me. The incarnation of the spirit they wanted so badly to spirit away. They hated me without ever having met me. But they were at the end of their tether then. A friend told me that a few minutes later they were having a perfectly calm discussion.

In the end nobody raised a finger against me, though a few friendly hands set me in the direction of the car. To picture myself being beaten I had to be pushed to the brink. Then again, my meekness is proverbial, and I'm often called naive and foolish. I wonder why I'm the one they've made the enemy again. Last year there were fewer rabble-rousers and they made less noise. This was still a minor stir, but it was indicative of the kind of hysteria that can ensue when a crowd reaches critical mass. In the space of a few hours I was both bearer of glad tidings and the devil's emissary, though all I did was unburden myself of a speech and stroll around the city to see what else was going on.

After a shot of vodka in a bar, Károly and I looked in on

László Rajk, who was kept at home by a leg injury. We talked
about Károly's stuffed cabbage, which he makes with eggs, lard,
and marjoram. My eyes nearly popped when I heard that.

Many people think that the government will use the up-
in-arms have-nots as unpaid auxiliaries, a kind of violent reserve
unit just waiting to be pressed into action. This is a new factor
and cannot be ignored. In certain countries the bureaucracy is
in collusion with the underworld. Cheap hit men gun down
intellectuals and human rights activists, then vanish into thin
air, at least the police don't seem able to find them. We haven't
yet reached that point, but the alarmists among us—and they
are legion—see us heading in that direction. I did not face such
hatred under Communism. Officials found it interesting to run
into dissidents at a play or concert. The secret police, too,
showed us a certain respect: they did their homework and read
what we wrote. We had an impact on them. They would try
sheepishly to justify their actions, distance themselves from
their roles. I have not met many people who hate me without
knowing me and make a show of their hatred.

Several days have passed. The fact that I went to Freedom
Square and had a close call shocked people for a while. Now
I'm back in the country, walking through the hills, though at
times I vanish and resurface on the TV screen. People smile:
they've seen me. The response to the incident has not yet died
down. Jutka tells me I've had a lot of calls from people inquiring
after my physical and psychological well-being.

I can't say this makes me happy; I don't like being a celeb-
rity, too well known to be roughed up. On the other hand I'm
upset by the thought that my renown might prompt an occasional lunatic to come to ritual grips with the past. I could

serve as the evil spirit he's been looking for. Victim for some, demon for others. I shake my head.

One television reporter asked me, "How is it you've gone from private dissident number one under Kádár to public enemy number one under Antall?" He wanted me to discuss it with him on camera, but I refused: I didn't find the subject particularly uplifting.

Sitting here on a log bench with a bottle of Italian Riesling next to me, I can only laugh at having seemed Satan incarnate to those men. Twenty years ago I kept an ax at the foot of my bed every night. Now I have a sharp knife within reach. I suppose I should stay out of sight for a while, but things always calm down and no one here in the country is going to bash my brains in. They're more likely to invite me down to their wine cellars for a drink. Though walking through the hills is intoxicating enough.

1992

To the Editorial Board of the Magyar Hírlap *(The Hungarian News)*,

*On Being Elected One of the Eleven Most Trustworthy
People in Hungary*

Dear Colleagues:

Thanks for the high marks. I'll do my best to remain worthy of them with exemplary conduct and diligence. Your choices are first-rate, though why isn't there a single woman on the list? A trustworthy eleven, a winning team, though. I'm not quite sure what you mean by trustworthy and what your criteria are. Trustworthy scales don't let you down; they give accurate weight. Trustworthy people don't let you down; they say what they mean (though let's stick to what they say in public, because what they say in the privacy of their homes doesn't concern us).

Your list brings together a number of memorable faces, all of which have one thing in common: they're their own men and deeply involved in one project or another. Cowboy types, yet not loners. No, nice fellows. Though there's something quirky about them: you can't make them do what they don't want to. This country still has a few like that, people who don't let you down, who are no good at being what they're not, and who keep the Ten Commandments with more or less success and fewer or greater qualms.

Murderers, liars, and thieves—I've seen them all, and let me tell you: they're a big bore. Shove a weapon into their hands and they'll kill. Tell them it's in their interest and they'll lie. Leave your wallet unattended and they'll take it. They're like Pavlov's dogs: programmed. They can't give themselves orders. Self-discipline is less predictable, more dramatic, more entertaining.

You do what you do and say what you say if you feel it's decent, right. If it's not, you don't do it, you don't say it, even if a thunderbolt will strike you dead or there's a noose around your neck. And you go on like that for decades without running off at the mouth about it. There's nothing to it but to do it.

We don't know who's right. We think we are, but we know they think *they* are. Sometimes we're on opposite sides, sometimes on the same side. Experienced players respect one another.

We need political parties. Has there ever been a democracy without them? Certain "independents" in the post-1990 sense of the word are discovering they liked the Party and are sick of parties. Go on smearing parties and you'll be stuck with the Party again.

The people we associated with in the democratic opposition were people we trusted. They never told us what to write or what not to write. They listened attentively and then had their say. Our dialogues were nothing if not civil—civilized, even.

In answer to your question: No, I'm not gearing up for

anything in particular. Sufficient unto the day is the evil thereof. (When people ask me questions, I try and answer them: my diploma says I'm a secondary schoolteacher.)

Not lying is not enough. If you think something is true and writing is your trade, then write it. And once you've written it, make sure it gets into print.

We gamble with fate in all kinds of ways. We all lose, of course, but the thing is to lose in style. I weigh a decision many times over on a trustworthy scale to make sure I won't be ashamed of my yesterday tomorrow. Whether others agree with me is less important than whether I agree with myself.

1992

To Hungarian Serbs and Croats

(Speech Delivered on the Steps of the Greek Catholic Chapel in Budapest, 26 September 1992)

Southern Slavs of Hungary, Serbs and Croats!

When a weapon takes a life, an infinitely complex piece of existence ceases to exist because of an absurdly simple flick of the finger.

When one human being shoots another, he is shooting God in the face.

- Who can rejoice at shooting God in the face?

Do you think it matters what the victim's name is, sex is, religion is, nationality is?

No murder is more gentle than any other, no murder more just than any other.

A person may have a motive or a compulsion to kill; no person has a moral right to kill.

A bullet is not a ball to be returned as in a game of tennis. The suffering this war has caused cannot be neutralized or justified by any form of government.

The politicians involved have addressed lesser evils by

139

resorting to greater evils, and the simpleminded have followed them.

Each side has had its passionate say, and each side believes it is in the right and has defended itself.

Observing from a distance blurs details but gives a less biased view of the whole.

The great misfortune currently afflicting this part of the world is a common historical phenomenon: knights in shining ideology, the braggarts of national intolerance, have led their followers into the fray like rams leading lambs to the slaughter, and once the blows begin they slip away and leave their followers to be mown down.

You are watching the fate of your brothers and sisters from a country where brothers and sisters are not at war.

No one who blesses a weapon is a priest.

A priest who fails to seek understanding with believers of other faiths is a godless priest.

Making peace is a creative act on a level with artistic creativity: it makes the coarse fine.

The peacemaker hands down the first and primary commandment: Thou shalt not kill.

The South Slavs will go on living together for centuries— if not in the same village, then in the same region.

With whom are they to work if not one another? With whom are they to trade if not one another? And they did so. But now they have surrounded themselves with walls of corpses and bred visions of mistrust, revenge, and terror.

They thought they were acting like patriots. They thought killing and being killed was self-sacrifice. They were wrong.

Self-sacrifice is a lifetime of serving others.

Serving your brothers and sisters by making peace is what

the Nazarene would have you do. And aiding refugees, no matter what side they are fleeing.

People on the other side of the border may urge you to take sides. Do not take sides.

Do not incite the refugees against anyone.

Hungarians are forbidden to support either side in this civil war.

We must send medicine, house the homeless, bring together people still capable of carrying on a dialogue. We must calm people down, sober them up. That in itself is enough.

Anyone who aids and abets killing on either side is a war criminal.

People capable of reason must restrain people blinded by passion, but to do so takes wisdom and courage.

Snapshot on the Day After
All Saints' Day

I am writing these lines on the Monday following All Saints' Day as a kind of retrospective on the immediate past.

Yesterday evening we had ten children and even more parents in to celebrate my son József's fifth birthday. My wife Judit received high praise for her cake. József's six-year-old brother Áron did not at all regret giving József his red bicycle as a present: he will get a bigger white one. We might even say that Áron was the real winner on József's birthday. Whatever pain accompanied the transaction has been put into words and is now a thing of the past. The two of them came to the agreement themselves after fair, bilateral negotiation and announced the decision to their mother at what was nothing if not a press conference. They also dealt with the succession of the bicycle József had grown out of.

The political concerns currently in the public eye make it clear that fifty-year-olds cannot do what five-year-olds can.

High-handed and egotistical, they reject all attempts at compromise.

Talking about politicians is in fashion nowadays, but people are careful, almost finicky about what they say. Only if their criticism targets the democratic opposition as well as the government can they be sure of offending no one, especially no one on high.

The reason such considerations are crucial is that everyone's existence is currently in the balance. Yesterday there was talk of university examination committees checking the political reliability of the teaching staff and using the results to dismiss some and hire others. Everywhere I look I see new appointments. If a new man takes over a state publishing house, I can be certain it will not publish my books—though I can be equally certain another publishing house will.

A woman at the birthday party reported that the mood in her office was very bad: her colleagues were afraid of jeopardizing their children's future, and some were looking for jobs abroad. I had to understand that these people during the brutal forties and fifties were either not yet born or mere children, and that if I found the prospects less terrifying than they did, it was because I had been through it all before. They did not want to go through it. The other young mothers agreed. Did I think there would be a war? No? Not with the Slovaks or Romanians or Serbs? Could the neofascists come to power? In a gradual putsch, for instance. People were saying the authorities didn't seem particularly upset by a demonstration with Nazi insignia against the president of the Republic. Was one branch of state power opposed to the other?

Are the new government's secret police and commandos

the same as before? What sort of orders are they given? A government official has stated that if things get worse and there is a general strike against the government, martial law will be declared. That means shelving the spring 1994 elections, which the latest public opinion polls say would remove the rightist coalition from office. No matter where in the country I go, people ask me anxiously whether everything the government does isn't aimed at preventing the 1994 elections from taking place.

On television this morning a member of Parliament and spokeswoman for the Arrow Cross skinheads came out against the Catholic Bishopric's recent pronouncement condemning anti-Semitism and racial hatred. She is a member of the leading government party.

People are talking about the Budapest-based initiative, released last week by a group of Hungarian and foreign writers, for the formation of an international democratic charter, one part of which at least would highlight the situation in East European societies.

What will follow Communism? Democracy or something else? The system we had between the wars? A frantic national radicalism granting rank, position, and state capital to the most trustworthy, that is, the most nationalist of its followers, who would be done in by professional competition?

When everything is in flux, when character-in-aspic is the specialty of the house, we need something less gelatinous, something constant and stable to hold on to. Why not try holding on to one another?

Although there are still leaves on the trees, we ramble through the rainy, acrid smell of leaf mold. The restaurants are humming, the streets in the center of town teeming with young people drinking straight from the bottle because they can't afford café prices. The roads are filled with large Western cars, especially in the vicinity of nouveau riche restaurants. More and more fathers are taking their children to kindergarten: their wives still have jobs.

Plan after plan is pouring in with a ring of the phone or knock on the door. People not used to being together feel the need to meet and talk and are therefore on their best behavior. Theaters, bookshops, clubs, libraries, universities, student groups, community centers, and coffee houses are sponsoring the sorts of programs that last year seemed to be losing their audiences and this year are attracting full houses. Good art is one remedy for anxiety, civilized forms of communication a bulwark against dialogue-phobic bluster.

The village where I withdraw to do my writing has finished bringing in the grape harvest. It's been a dry summer; there will be less wine, but it will be better. Even when the main street is quiet, as it is now, people have a friendly word for one another. There are no angry people here. Their sober humor stays with them when they have their glass of wine. It's a hard life, a hand-to-mouth life, but they cope. The people who kept rabbits before are trying goats now. Some of the craftsmen have more time to spend with their families. Couples dance till dawn at the church fair. A lonely old woman can expect her younger neighbors to look in on her two or three times a day. What my neighbors look forward to most is gathering their families around a groaning board on a name day or holiday—and that they manage to do. When somebody dies, the whole village shows up at the funeral. They grumble over their incomes, but wouldn't dream of moving. Gazing down at the lake from the terraces of the huts where they press their grapes, they must feel they have the most beautiful countryside in Hungary and even in the world (by now they've been on bus tours to Venice). They listen to the news and by and large accept what they hear me say on television. My local political opponent is a good man; we've always been on friendly terms.

Last week I arrived half frozen from Warsaw and left immediately for Pécs. I gave one talk to an audience of several hundred in a provincial school auditorium and another, the day before yesterday, at a cultural center on the outskirts of Budapest. The day after tomrrow I have a question-and-answer session at the University of Debrecen and then a week's respite from my itinerant teaching. If no major calamity comes up, that is.

1992

Hedonists of the Brain

How do we writers get on with one another? Very well, thank you.

Except that writers have no "we." All my colleagues cultivate their own way of doing things. No one represents a pattern for anyone else, though we can learn a thing or two from one another. We are all masters at play and of play, self-publishers and self-promoters, close-mouthed palaverers, hedonists of the brain. Having the knack of putting ourselves into other people's skins and minds, we go beyond what is normally said.

I've met a great many writers in my day. An interesting crowd, actually, quite engaging. We may pick on one another, but we do think we're fascinating. Each of us is a challenge to all of us: What if their way is better than mine? Though after a while it stops being an issue: I have a different way and that's all there is to it. We grow more and more self-indulgent.

I admire my colleagues for their peculiarities, but it is only if they can't pester me or foist themselves on me, only if I don't depend on them that we fall into conversation. And that's literature: falling into conversation. We like a good time and we're curious about one another. First the monkey-man withdraws into his corner, then he longs for crowds. He may turn into a teacher or a fireman for a time, but sooner or later he proves just another member of that supersensitive clan whose constant subject matter is the I and you and the we and you, thoughts of ourselves and others.

Writers are more than their collected works, they are the memory of their persons. We all live with a mythology of the world—with people we know and people we know only by reputation, with heroes and villains—and we are all one another's stories. I am the image my name evokes in others; you are the same. We are picture albums to be leafed through at random, at will.

Like anyone with a certain renown, writers have a mythic quality about them. (We always knew our teachers before they stepped into the classroom on the first day of school: their reputation had preceded them.) The speeches they give, the books they write, the conversations they have at mass meetings or in libraries for the blind—they all partake of one and the same essence.

We writers? I muse on the "we" one morning at the Writers Association, which happens to be choosing a new president. We writers certainly can make fools of ourselves. One candidate tells another with great warmth how happy he would be if the latter won. How childish, how elegant, how self-indulgent. There was a time when the politics in this country went on here and only here. Now there is politics everywhere but here.

All the excitement has gone out of this place. We are all mildly bored with one another.

The world no longer cares who says what here: the crucial matches are being played on other fields. We are merely up-holding the dignity of our craft. Many of us have had to accept a new status: the noble poor. Once-famous writers are willing to go without royalties so long as their books continue to appear. Appalled by the incongruity of the more-books-fewer-readers syndrome, even we have stopped reading. We are now like those disagreeable characters who come up to you on the street, grab you by the collar, and pour out whatever is on their mind.

Should writers, then, return to politics? Not necessarily. Though why not? Their spare time is their own. Some like to jog, some to teach, and some to play with their children. What if some enjoy dabbling in politics? Writers are full-fledged cit-izens. They are even likely to think more than the average citizen. Why shouldn't they have their say in matters of public concern? Why shouldn't they answer if someone asks their opinion? And if what they say is interesting, why shouldn't they be asked again? The answers they give to political questions may upset professional politicians—politicians in office are par-ticularly susceptible—and writers living in dictatorships can get into deep trouble. Even in democratic regimes they occasionally end up the butt of rude newspaper articles or anonymous letters, but that's bearable. There's no point wasting time on such things. You don't respond, you grow a thick skin, you don't let it get to you. When György Lukács learned that someone had been running him down in influential circles, his only response was, "They can hang me if they like. As long as I'm not there."

There are adventures to be had even in the most civilized

of conditions. Don't turn away any man, woman, or child who wants to speak to you. Just stay in your chair. Your battle is a spiritual, intellectual one. Jump on your steed and dash to the tourney if you like, but the arena is empty: the public is tired of yesterday's jousters; it wants something new to applaud.

Little David killed Goliath with the sling of literature. The stone takes years to reach its goal. Then comes the story of King David the perpetrator. The poet and sovereign can no longer hide behind the innocent shepherd boy: the poet-politician has entered the lists of responsibility; the tyrant-elect sloughs off his guerrilla skin.

Literature is a slow voice, like the whale's song: it is long vaults and encasements; it is loath to gabble or shout. The thought is neither friend nor foe to the deed; it is separate from it, describing it, understanding it, entering into it, making it its own. The writer is attracted more by understanding than by victory.

What are writers good at? They are reliable appraisers; they will tell you what a thing is. They are professional representers; they can sense a thing from the sanctity of their immediate presence. The past exists because writers re-present it. They are experts at bringing things into the present, at an ongoing metempsychosis. People take refuge in one another the better to understand one another. The reader takes refuge in the writer.

We writers are rarely "we." Even if we love everybody (which is impossible), we face our unwritten space alone. The world overpowers us. There are so many people out there. How can anyone claim we deal with the world from a position of strength?

We writers and the public? When you come down to it,

we're afraid of the public. At times we get carried away with people, but we soon have enough of them and air out our rooms when they leave. Then we withdraw entirely and cultivate their memory.

We know what it's like to be alone within the majority. We could rehearse our monotonous tales of indignity and persecution, but we won't: there are enough martyrs elbowing their way to pedestals as it is.

Now it's time to focus on the doers, the go-getters, time to make them acceptable, back them up with people to serve as tools for their success. Oh the indignities and frustrations of the naive desire for success!

If I am afraid of my contemporaries, it is because they have never known long-term, respectable success. Even now that they are getting on in years, they are unsure of themselves and hence aggressive: they set goals and push ahead, hoping to beat the competition or at least prove it wrong, but they keep getting tangled in a net of ulterior motives. I can never make out where I stand with them.

Writers write with their entire existence, with kith and kin more than pen and ink. Writers are as much writers when they gape or chatter as when they write. That writers are only what is on paper is a myth perpetrated by literary scholars to put us in their hands. But we don't care how easily approachable or carvable we are for them. If there is one thing we writers can agree upon, it is that we are not roast turkeys.

1992

The Meek Shall Inherit the Earth

*(Speech Given 31 January 1993 for the Bokor Catholic
Action Group, Which Set the Title)*

Seriously? Aren't children the first to starve to death or expire
in the gas chamber? And who is meeker than a child? Do the
meek command the violent or vice versa? Did being meek ever
make anyone rich and powerful? How are the meek the winners
when they are attacked or cheated? Do they fight back? Do
they defend themselves by arguing, suing, swinging their fists?
Aren't they the ones you see sneaking off with their tails between their legs or, at best, sadder but wiser?

Who are the meek, anyway? Do they really exist? As even
the most gentle poet will allow, the heart goes out to both the
tiger and the doe. And children aren't any different—I can
attest to that. Even the "meekest" of my four children—the
one who empathizes with everyone, the one who refuses to
accept death or irreparable loss—even he loves stories about
wild animals. And when the time comes to choose an animal
to turn into, which does he choose? The tiger.

Perhaps you think of yourselves, good Christians all, as

belonging to the privileged meek. Or if not yourselves, then your priest. Well, I can't say I've ever known a religious leader of any denomination to be particularly meek. No one who works with people—teachers, judges, politicians, psychiatrists—considers meekness a vocational advantage: everyone who works with people wants something from them—from members of the congregation, from the student body, from prisoners in the dock, from the sick and dying, even from faceless consumers and taxpayers; everyone beleaguers them with norms and expectations, spurs them on, holds them back, cultivates, prunes, and hoes them as a winegrower his vines, a gardener his lettuce.

I could cite parallels and parables galore, but the fact is, if you love your neighbor with no ulterior motive; if you have no desire to convert, redeem, or inspire; if you are content to accept things the way a passenger on a train registers a tree bursting into flower or struck by lightning, the way a writer like Gyula Krúdy observes a man eating and drinking at the table next to him, the way a person watches a stork on a chimney, tactfully, nonviolently, respecting rather than prying; if you are the sort of person who will speak out and help out when necessary but never impose yourself or your opinions on anybody and never suggest that you are specially qualified to distinguish good from evil by virtue of your philosophy, education, religion, or vocation; if after a long retreat you emerge from your cave without preaching to the general public and threatening the naysayers with fire and brimstone—then you are one of the truly rare examples of meekness, an attribute free of all institutional, organizational, occupational, or congregational ties and unattainable by joining or signing up for anything, you are unrecognized in the way a knight, saint, or doctor is recognized and unexplainable by any book or combination of books.

Yet the meek do exist. They may be midwives or bus drivers, they may even be popes—a certain number twenty-three, for instance—but they are hard to spot and altogether mysterious, because there is no accounting for how the doe tames the tiger, trains it to trot behind it like a kitten and breakfast on muesli instead of meat.

Don't be meek *because* you want to inherit the earth. Then why? Just because. Or, rather, to have the whole world at your fingertips, here and now. The bright sun on the snow, now. The crisp air in the field, now. The stray dogs coupling over by the ditch with what must be perfect moral equanimity, and the tiny pups that will come of it. The world conquerors you have read about, the world travelers—their empires and adventures are yours. Everything I see is mine, everyone I think of with affection is mine. The view from Chain Bridge or Saint George Hill is so beautiful, so satisfying that I can't begin to give it its due. But even just greeting a new day, taking a deep breath and stretching, pouring something nice and warm into your stomach, knowing that you can still move, that you haven't been downed by a bullet, thrombosis, or an oncoming car, that the horsemen of the Apocalypse have missed you this time round—even these things are enough to warrant thanks to Creation and Creator for being and letting you be, now, at this very moment.

But if snow glittering in the sun is mine, so is the latest catastrophe. Not only the empire is mine but the slavery that goes with it, not only the martyr but the hangman. Mine is the tank and the rocket that hits it, mine the oil slick and the tar-coated seagull; trickling truth and raging, commonplace lies; masterpiece and mass murder—I have inherited the earth with all its wonders and squalor.

The hustlers and rustlers, the social climbers and status seekers, the eager beavers and go-getters for whom nothing is ever enough, the insulted, the suspicious, and anyone bloated with a personal truth—these people may have failed to notice that the earth is theirs, here and now. Others inherit the earth simply by recognizing it as their own. Shall we call them meek? You don't need to go far to find them; you don't need to look them up in the encyclopedia. You may wake up every morning in the same bed with one or nod to one daily on the stairs.

The meek don't expect rewards for what they do. Why do they do it, then? Just because. Certainly not to inherit the earth. The earth is theirs, and they know it. They don't give charity so God will repay them; they don't help the weak so the great bookkeeper in the sky will credit their account. They leave the rewards of the Garden of Eden—the heavenly resort hotel where the hungry will gorge themselves at groaning boards and the lonely will ride arm in arm on gingerbread merry-go-rounds—to the tourist brochure.

If they don't expect rewards, if the earth is already theirs for the asking, then why do they do it?

I repeat. Just because.

Don't knock on secret's gate.

P.S. One more thing: we are all capable of attacking the meek.

1993

Central Europe Redivivus

No matter what we call it and whether or not we speak of it as such, Central Europe was, is, and probably will continue to be. Like the Danube, which existed long before it was called the Danube. Central Europe may well outlive us.

Its existence, its reality does not depend on Central European rhetoric; it does not depend on whether people speak good or ill of it, whether they think it beautiful or ugly, mysterious or dull, whether it happens to be in or out of fashion, whether its nations are contracting nuptials or engaging in warfare. It exists as the Balkans exist (at peace or at war) and the Middle East (whether or not the current Arab-Israeli peace talks bear fruit) and the Commonwealth of Independent States (whose ancient past includes both Tsarist Russia and the Soviet Union). Even the Austro-Hungarian Empire still exists, at least in pictures and in our mind's eye. It has been praised, criticized, and studied—though never quite to death. Regions, territories, and localities are sturdier than borders. States are preserved as ideas, but the Danube flowing and the peoples living along its banks are more than an idea.

The existence of Central Europe is thus a given. And yet Central Europe is transitory, provisional. It is neither east nor west; it is both east and west. It represents their mutual presence, all tension and irony: single-party habits and an attempt at pluralism; socialism and capitalism; state ownership and private ownership; the redistribution of wealth and the free market; state control and a civil society; paternalistic politics and a critical intelligentsia.

Central Europe is made up of small nations between two large ones: Germany and Russia. We small nations, living as we do within precarious, much debated, and occasionally redrawn borders, have restless collective egos and provisional, makeshift identities. We all seem to be expecting something, an explanation of where we belong. We tend to feel isolated, hence the bearers of a unique mission and naturally the victims and targets of plots by neighbors and international conspiracies.

Central Europe is thus both utopia and chimera, and while some of our poets have treated it as a feverish vision, it is also a reality. We are not particularly eager to acknowledge the reality, however, because we would rather see ourselves as a more noble twin, an image from a golden age. In other words, we have maintained certain internal paradoxes and are unwilling to excise them with the either/or logic of the scapel. Glorious myths and tragic anniversaries get our blood up even after centuries. Nations living so close together apparently need to justify their existence with origin myths and their ailing contemporary reality with historical rationalizations.

But if we are dissatisfied with our current governments, we must recognize that they have not come from without, that they have not been imposed upon us by the superpowers; they are the result of what is in us, they are our own creation. If we are plagued by malicious, isolationist, high-handed policies, they are our own doing, the realization of our own ideas. The great challenge we face is living side by side: developing a common system of values, establishing a neighborly ethic and sticking to it. Our region requires an ability to get along with others. We must accept our neighbors just as we accept fellow passengers on a train. Like it or not, we will be waking up in their presence tomorrow and the day after.

Gestures of coming together and making peace are in order every day of the year. An in-depth knowledge of the history of the peoples in question will go far to temper our aggressivity and help us to find our own place in the scheme of things. What seem like hostile policies may well stem from distorted views of the past. When nationalism kills, it has deep roots in people's psyches.

Although national identity cannot be seen with the naked eye, it shows in the way a nation's villages, towns, and cities resemble one another. The same holds for our supranational, Central European identity. Throughout the region there are streets, whole districts indistinguishable from one another. In the past few years our rundown cities have been receiving a face-lift: public buildings have been repaired, churches restored. The goal is to make the cities look more like their Western counterparts; instead they look more like one another. Central Europe also implies similar images, smells, personal relationships, and types of behavior, none of which will please certain cocksure nationalists, for whom all comparatists are brazen liars. I would maintain that a society should be able to look itself in the mirror and find family resemblances. It is something like required reading or a yearly visit to an aunt: it may be annoying, but there is also something uplifting about it.

Many feel let down by what is happening in Central Europe today, especially after the euphoria of the early days. I must say I have not experienced extremes of either intoxication or sobriety. I see what people are trying to do, but do not believe in miracles. Gravity is still a potent force, and we have not improved our petulant, irascible nature.

Whether Central Europe, as it is, is a beautiful or ugly place is another question. I will say only that its mixture of east and west is truly unique and truly validates the Central European idea. I may choose to call every house I've lived in beautiful even if some were far from it. In the same way those of us who live here may wish to call Central Europe beautiful.

Foreigners who come to us as tourists see its beauty. They also sense certain common characteristics in our railway stations and restaurants, our spas and bureaucratic institutions. There are even strange people who return to our countries every summer, tourist missionaries of sorts (though they are not ascetics by any means and simply find Central Europe to their liking), people who respond to names like Mariánské Lázně, Zakopane, the Tatras, Lake Balaton, appreciating what they have to offer. Such people take our cohesion for granted and find attempts to destroy it unnatural. In their own way they are further proof that Central Europe exists. We might say, then, that tourists have as much to contribute to the debate over Central Europe as politicians.

There is also much independent, transpolitical exchange —cultural and economic—among Central Europeans themselves. People come and·go, bring things and take things, have conferences and business meetings, eat and drink together.

Central Europe is thus created more by universities and publishers, theaters and schools, studios and travel agencies than
by the statements of highly placed officials. The exchange takes
place even if not provided for in the state plan. Political integration will come at a later stage, the result of more intense
contact.

Central Europe is an aristocratic metaphor. One cannot
rant and rave under its flag. Its relationship to reality is mental,
not militant. I do not see throngs of voters gathering in its
name, nor do I see much political or economic advantage to
integration in the immediate future. Prospects further down the
line are promising, but politicians tend to rush things.

And Central Europe is an intellectual concept. Intellectuals
have headed nation-states and represented their interests, but
I maintain that we must distinguish between the interests of
intellectuals and the interests of nation-states. A thinking person does not have to defend any interests, bend before any
definitive truth, pledge a priori loyalty to any absolute principle.
The nation-state is just another tempting, supposedly righteous
idea.

Is Central Europe a utopia? Opinions on the matter differ
enormously. One extreme maintains that the nation-state is
the ultimate good and any limitation of its sovereignty must be
made only for the sake of the European Union and NATO.
Which is the mirror image of yesterday's dogma, namely, that
the nation-state is the ultimate good and its sovereignty may
be limited only for the sake of Comecon and the Warsaw Pact.
The difference is that while the countries of East-Central Europe were members of the latter two organizations, they are still
knocking at the doors of the former two. Furthermore, their
disappointment is growing—independent of national and po-

litical differences—because all they get from even the most forthcoming Western politicians are halfhearted promises: We are willing to let our eastern neighbors into the anteroom but no farther. The former east-bloc countries, convinced that integration is essential to their interests, have proposed a series of steps or trials in the direction of membership, but all they receive for their pains is the noncommittal *mañana*.

Like all unequal relationships this state of frustrated expectation may go on indefinitely. It is a kind of unrequited love that actually suits both sides. "Now! Now!" says the East. "No! No!" says the West. But a snubbed eastern suitor can take solace in the belief that his neighbors have met with even worse treatment and that he has relatively better prospects. The suitors are thus engaged in an ongoing competition over who will be the first to escape the scrap heap where President Havel sees the signatories of the Visegrád Treaty residing. We wait for the call, looking straight ahead of us and communicating with one another in only the most neutral terms. We want to keep our passion pure.

But what if the long wait gives rise to other possibilities? What if the countries involved, tired of being seduced and abandoned, start accepting other invitations to the dance? They will begin by flirting with one another and move on to the United States, Japan, the Commonwealth of Independent States, or the Near East, with nary a thought of polygamy. All the areas in question have an interest in a foothold in Central Europe—behind Germany's back, as it were—and thus have no interest in the precipitous integration of our region into the European Union. Perhaps Central Europe will find its sovereignty in such multilateral relationships; perhaps Central Europeans will not be able to live together until they stop battling over integration. If the much coveted marriage to fair Europa fails to come off, there are other fair maidens waiting in the wings. This is not the first time we have been put off by our friends.

The European Union and NATO belong together, and since integration implies mutual trust and economic, cultural, political, and military reliability, the neutral EFTA countries will be sacrificing their neutrality by joining. They may think twice about it, especially after the Russians have hinted they are not particularly happy with the prospect even now: a nation's geopolitical interests tend to outlast its political system. And only when the neutral countries do join will the post-Communist countries have their turn.

Not that we are a particularly attractive prospect. Do we accept Yugo romanticism? Of course not. Do we accept tooth-and-nail ethnic relations and the concomitant border disputes? Heaven forbid. Do we say, "Protect us until we pounce on one another"? Let's just refrain from pouncing on one another.

Once the European Union accepts Austria, Austria may whisper to us over her shoulder to hide under her skirts. We won't all fit. No, German-speaking Europe will be on one side of the customs barrier and we'll be on the other. Still, our neighbors will be interested in us, each in its own way. Austria—given emotional ties, tradition, benefits, and design—will maintain as much of a connection with us as joining the European Union will allow her to. Everyone wants to serve as a bridge for trade with the eastern market, and this is the time to prepare for it.

While there may have been any number of clandestine dreams about a union of Austrians with Czechs, Slovaks, Hungarians, Croats, and Slovenes—that is, with the nations of the

Monarchy—there has been no public proposal of same. The division of Yugoslavia into Catholic and Orthodox segments has proved more complex than anyone could have imagined, and what is left of the rest of Central and Southwestern Europe is a north-south strip including the former people's democracies minus East Germany but plus the Baltic countries, all of which, as I have said, are nervously competing for first place in the eyes of the European Union.

And if nobody wins? Or everybody at once in some intricate, half-baked measure? Western politicians must be aware that by dividing the population into categories they will only exacerbate existing tensions and instability. I presume, then, that it will be all or none. All? Isn't that an awful lot? Then unfortunately it may have to be none.

At least we must consider the possibility. We won't make it go away by not talking about it. And if it does come to pass, it will be a strong argument for another kind of integration: Central European integration. Not so much to turn us all into winners as to help us support one another through hard times and preserve a modicum of sovereignty in the face of one or another powerful neighbor. Besides, proving that we can work together and with the world makes us more attractive, riper, for pan-European integration.

Optimism in this context means refusing to let the object of our concern, Central Europe, follow a path not of its own choosing; it means seeing our future open before us, a future dependent only upon our own wishes, our own work, our own selves.

1993

What Makes a Hungarian?

Having been one, or becoming one, or being one today. Having a Hungarian education, history, way of doing things. Feeling part of the cultural and political nation. Calling yourself a Hungarian (or hyphenated Hungarian).

What makes a Hungarian? The world of memories associated with "Hungaria," which includes many ethnic communities, elements assimilated and elements adapted, and the dowry that has come with them. The entire corpus of "Hungarica," that is, every text written in Hungarian and every text, written here or elsewhere, about Hungarians. Every thought anywhere in the world—on the Hungarian Plain, in the Himalayas—that anyone has ever had about us. Every event bearing on Hungarians, as long as it has left a trace or at the very least continues to exist in the memory of the Almighty (if He is doing His duty, and we hope He is, as Eternal Archivist). Every manifestation of yourself, your every piece of wisdom and stupidity, everything that makes you proud and makes you blush, everything you have read and heard, believed and rejected—as long as you are Hungarian. Every piece of mail with a Hungarian stamp or address. The dreadful torrent of words recorded by the super-tappers who forced and entered Hungarian telephone conversations as a third ear. The houses Hungarians live in and things they use anywhere on earth. The motions of Hungarians at work, play, and loggerheads, in love and in their cups as captured by a ubiquitous candid camera. In other words, a reality of inconceivable variety about which only a total ass would presume to make blanket statements. Something with as many definitions as people with opinions on the subject. Something you can go on about forever, if such is your pleasure—but it is more. It is saints and rapists, heroes and traitors, geniuses and idiots—you name it. Including the sort of people who ask, "What makes a Hungarian?"

You will search in vain for a term analogous to *magyarság* (Hungarians collectively, the Hungarian nation) in, say, English or French. English has only "the English," French only "les français." They know there is great diversity within their nations; they pride themselves on it.

Every definition is literature, so the only answer to the question "What makes a Hungarian?" is a literary one, and I would broaden its scope to include the whole of Hungarian literature and beyond: all the material in the National Library.

The first step, however, is to eliminate all value judgments and normative designations, be they flattering or disparaging. Brave? There are brave Hungarians and cowardly Hungarians. No one can calculate the proportion. Hungarians are truthful and deceitful, beautiful and ugly, generous and parsimonious, hospitable and aloof, tender and ruthless.

Can a single definition cover everything we do, everything

we are? Why even bother to ask? The very question prompts
another, namely, what is wrong with the people who ask such
a question? Who would substitute a paragraph or article for an
endless reading list?

Collective emotions (like pride and shame) and family sensibilities and hatreds may make for interesting novels, but what
reality is there in emotional myths?

Albanians are more optimistic about the future than we
Hungarians, but we would never change places with them. We
may plot apocalypses at night, but in the morning we get up
and go to work. And we know how to work: our achievements
and general level of accomplishment prove that. Look us up in
the yearbooks of international statistics.

We are basically identified with what we produce and consume, what we buy and sell. We are the writings, paintings,
musical performances, observations, calculations, and com-
munications we present to the outside world; we are our every
export; we are even the things we cannot manage to sell.

If a Hungarian is a conglomeration of elements that cannot
be embraced, that supersedes all individual elements, the conglomeration should be taken not as a separate thing but the
sum total of all its texts and actions. Anyone who tries to distill
it turns it into something abstract and false, a kind of kitsch,
something that may still pass for wisdom in a school composition
but is totally useless in any other context.

Which of the myriad classic novels by Jókai or Krúdy should
you choose to answer the question? Clearly, singling out one
would be arbitrary. And why Jókai and Krúdy? Why not a
recently completed manuscript by an as yet unknown young
man or woman writing in Hungarian?

If you ask what makes a Hungarian, you may end up like

the pupil who asked his master what the tao is. When the master ignored the question, the pupil asked again. Again the master ignored it. The third time, however, the response came as a sudden blow on the back. The essence of the blow was more "What I do" than a punishment. And "What I do" is quite close to "What I am." What makes you a Hungarian is being true to yourself, giving the gift of your individuality— the way you handle a baby, the way you handle a sentence— to your nation. What makes you a patriot is that you are *not* like others. Then what are you like? Yourself.

Jewish Hungarians, German Hungarians, Slovak Hungarians, American Hungarians, Swedish Hungarians, Japanese Hungarians make a gift of their Jews, Germans, Slovaks, Americans, Swedes, and Japanese to the Hungarians. Everyone has made a contribution; everyone has something to contribute.

The question is how broad or narrow Hungarians are in their conception of themselves. When they're in a tight spot, they're narrow and suspicious; they burrow into a bunker and kick out anybody who isn't Hungarian enough for them. And who qualifies as Hungarian is determined by examination on the part of experts from a self-appointed clan of quintessential Hungarians. To which all I can say is, "Ha!" I always thought a good Hungarian was someone who managed to enhance the image of Hungary here and abroad.

The self-shrinking national strategy takes what it considers non-national and delights in condemning it. The self-expanding national strategy takes anything from the outside world that can be fruitfully related to what was previously considered national and delights in integrating the two. I use the word "strategy" because I find the concept of 'national strategy' more valid than that of 'national identity.' The latter is static, enigmatic, hard to pin down, while a strategy is visible in terms of action. We all have conscious or unconscious 'life strategies'; in other words, our actions are metaphorically interconnected.

History consists of the tracks made by strategy and includes the risks players take, whether they win or lose. Players with promise analyze their losses, learn from them, and try to work out more effective strategies. Both individual and collective action may be mere play as far as fate is concerned, but in our neck of the woods lazy minds use "fate" as a coverup for fault.

There is an alternative to faulty action, to the kind that ends in defeat. Action can end in success, after all. The minds that restyle their faults as fate are the heroes of the self-shrinking strategy and the nemesis of the connection-making strategy. Don't bite off more than you can chew. Stop going on so much about what is and not national and start living. Then you can say in passing, "I belong to my nation."

Which is correct. Because what belongs to my nation is what I am. And that, ladies and gentlemen, is something we can all claim for ourselves. So before we start racking our brains yet again over what makes a Hungarian, let me suggest that we simply stand in front of our mirrors. At last being a Hungarian means I being me, you being you, and so on. No one is authorized to say you are, you are not, you are, you are not, you step to the right, you step to the left, and that group—over there.

The strategy that goes looking for enemies may be viable, but when it works it leads to war. Its logic is the logic of escalation; it fairly forces the players onto the field of battle.

The broad-minded strategy—or, if you like, the generous national strategy—is also viable, but it presupposes that all the players are broad-minded and generous, that they are willing to take the initiative, that they prefer the art of enterprise to reactive grousing. This city and this country tend more towards the former, towards giving and taking and making connections.

When I come down from my literary high, I see the practical Hungarian more than the tragic one. In the West, too, I hear the joke about a Hungarian being someone who follows you into a revolving door and comes out ahead of you. As I say, our nights are for apocalyptic jam sessions, our days for work. Whenever I look tragic—especially if I seem to be enjoying it—my wife makes fun of me.

Moods change, of course. I am glad there are as many moods as types of weather. As you are aware, fluctuations within the seasons and variations in the transition from one to the next represent a rich strain in Hungarian literature.

And so, my much esteemed fellow Hungarians, let us give Now its due, and if we feel like playing the saint, then let us sanctify the fleeting moment, which smuggles something of the rapture of existence into our everyday lives and is to the school of death as the opening of eyes is to the closing of eyes.

By so doing we may consider our patriotic duty done.

By so doing? Well, not exactly. By having lived a greater or lesser part of our lives here. We must live according to our lights and use the dual apprenticeship of freedom and solidarity to come to grips with our anxieties. Which is also my answer to the question of what makes a Hungarian.

1993

Eternally Waiting

Can Jews remain in East-Central Europe? That is the question.

Hungary has between eighty and a hundred thousand Jews, Romania about twenty thousand, the rest of the countries a few thousand each. Jews have had several waves of opportunity to emigrate from their Central European homelands, and many have taken advantage of them; indeed, in some instances the vast majority has left.

A good half of Hungary's Holocaust survivors left the country. Those still here have chosen to remain. Most are elderly now and may feel too helpless to make the move, but they were not elderly after the war. Nor is there any general, precipitous movement toward emigration at present—nothing comparable to the Soviet Jews' *aliya*, for instance—though some young scholars and highly qualified experts are quietly taking up positions outside the country, usually claiming it is only for the time being.

The vast majority of Central European Jewry has decided

to wait. Wait and see. If constitutional democracy takes hold in Central Europe, if the relationship of the state to the individual and to minorities is liberal, if society tolerates plurality because society itself is becoming more heterogeneous, then the Jews will stay. If not, they will dwindle—in waves again, perhaps—though a few will always remain behind to take care of the synagogue, the cemetery, the written records of their presence in the region.

In other words, the answer to the question depends not so much on the Jews as on the circumstances. The "Jewish question" is not a question of Jews. If the ruling spirit is one in which civil liberties thrive, the very otherness of the few Jews left will make them a valued segment of their societies, in which case, yes, even immigration *to* Central European metropolises is conceivable! We must keep the alternatives in mind. Jews who leave have few possibilities to choose from.

Let me expand on this point. Ours is a decade in which, to my mind, democracy will take root in Central Europe. I do not see the other option—nationalist dictatorships, which Central European Jews would hardly find propitious—gaining ground. The rhetoric of the radical, jingoist right against neighboring countries or ethnic groups, against representatives of the former Communist regime, and against the three-headed monster of America plus (to simplify matters slightly) the World Bank plus (most dangerous of all) international Jewry has failed to impress most Central Europeans. Rather than radical passions and passionate irrationality what I find is mild optimism and a rejection of extremes at either end of the spectrum.

The pendulum that swung to the right is now swinging to the left, and in the more stable societies the center will slow it down. All former spiritual and intellectual isms have come alive again—nothing can be buried indefinitely—but none has been able to predominate for any length of time, none has gained absolute sway. Too much is going on; things are changing too fast. Even an institution as venerable and venerated as the Catholic Church has lost some of its authority in Poland because it has demanded too much and refused to make do with a partial say.

Given the many possibilities that have opened up in Central Europe—the proliferation of lifestyles, the transformation of the economy, the revitalization of the city—I would call pluralization the main tendency. The middle class is growing in legal leaps and illegal bounds, the professional class is developing nicely, and a new elite—which is, naturally enough, not a hundred-percent new—is taking shape. Now that the populace has been granted certain civil liberties, it will be loath to give them up in the name of an idea, any idea, be it socialism, the nation, or Christianity. Neocollectivist leanings though there be, they are particularly incompatible with the new pluralism: the young find individualist routes to self-realization far more attractive than uniforms and slogans. The main trend is very definitely *embourgeoisement*, the growth of the middle class. Moderate, dependable, sober voices tend to inspire the most sympathy.

The western rim of what used to be Eastern Europe is moving quickly in the direction of complete integration with Western Europe—military included—but it still needs to prove its reliability by satisfying certain ironclad conditions—by demonstrating tolerance and self-control, for example. Once it has done so, the organic coupling of its social consciousness with Western values will gradually follow. If Warsaw, Cracow, Prague, Brno, Bratislava, Ljubljana, and Budapest turn into vibrant, open cities—and they are moving in the right direction—the natural flow of traffic, virtually independent of the degree of institutional involvement, will create the necessary common European norms. In such an atmosphere Jews can easily find a place.

This optimistic prognosis holds definitely for the region that includes the cities I have just mentioned, and guardedly, with certain time constraints, for Eastern Europe proper: the former Soviet republics, Romania, and the Balkans. I believe that the maelstrom raging in the former Yugoslavia—the Bosnia Syndrome, we might call it—will serve more as deterrent than temptation for the former communist bloc. An ethnic civil war requires a checkered array of ethnic groups, a mountainous terrain, a long tradition of guerrilla warfare, and a cult of the armed hero. Such a combination exists only in the Balkans.

If there is anything Central Europeans do not want, it is what we see coming from the Balkans on the evening news. We could theorize forever about the differences between the internal conflicts in the former Yugoslavia and the former Soviet Union, but the fact remains that the Russians' strategy differs fundamentally from the Serbs', if only because the proportions are different. It makes no sense to equate the relationship between the Russians and Ukrainians with the relationship between the Serbs and Croats. The Bosnia Syndrome is not contagious. The Caucasus did not learn to shoot from the Balkans; the Caucasus began shooting before the Balkans. True, there are a great many groups active in the area, but the hysterical ones are in the minority, and the center is pushing the worst of them to the sidelines.

Of course East-Central Europe has now and will continue to have a radical right either openly proclaiming anti-Semitic programs or not. But that right is closely related in mentality and logic to a sporadically reappearing neofascism, whose audience never exceeds ten percent of the population and often falls below it. It thus attracts proportionally the same size audience as in Western Europe. In the former Soviet republics and Southeast Europe, where the political situation is even more amorphous than in Central Europe, the percentage of the population susceptible to neofascist phraseology hovers between twenty and twenty-five. So irresolute a mass still seeking an identity might well succumb to a modern fascist movement: it is inexperienced in representational democracy, and its sympathies slide back and forth across the political spectrum.

One response to extremism is a strong-arm, strong-president democracy (with its mix of nationalist and democratic phraseology) that countenances a modicum of pluralism and refrains from attacks on minorities. It also refrains from anti-Semitic rhetoric, though it all but invites the media to make use of it. The other response is a solid, constitutional, parliamentary democracy that determines on the basis of a consensus among conservatives, liberals, and socialists what is and is not to be tolerated.

Even though Eastern Europe is experiencing a certain disappointment and even skepticism vis-à-vis the West, neither the radical right nor the "old-new" communists have been able to come up with anything better than multiparty, constitutional democracy and a market economy. And because both right and left need representation in Parliament, they are forced to conform to parliamentary custom and logic. I do not consider the Weimar parallel valid: a landslide victory for the right is nothing less than phantasmagorical. The history-book images of Nazi Germany are as much a deterrent as the television-screen images of Bosnia. The players have learned their lesson. The powers that be are cautious; they have none of the radical populists' enthusiasm and no interest in supporting neofascist adventurists.

I well understand the risk involved in making optimistic prognoses. Nor am I unaware of worse- and worst-case scenarios. I realize that Western Europe may not gratify Central Europe's desire to enter its Union within the foreseeable future and that if the resulting resentment causes an identity crisis among Central Europeans, it may lead to the reestablishment of authoritarian state structures (though backed this time by nationalist rather than socialist rhetoric).

Nationalist rhetoric must inevitably choose between a territorial and therefore political definition of the nation or an ethnic and therefore religious one. While the former may not necessarily discriminate against the Jew, the latter will be obliged to. If to be considered Hungarian, for instance, one must not only live in Hungary, be a Hungarian citizen, and speak Hungarian, if to be considered Hungarian one must satisfy two further criteria, namely, be a Christian (because Hungary is by definition a Christian nation) and the scion of an old Hungarian family; if, in other words, the definition of "Hungarian" takes us into the murky waters of ethnic origins, if the ethnic concept of nationality triumphs over the political—then the conflict between majority and minority will intensify and the ensuing brand of religious nationalism will sooner or later compel Jews to leave. (One can obviously replace "Hungarian" here with the name of any nation in East-Central Europe.)

Going even farther afield—though not straying from our topic—I would point out that the State of Israel, like its Middle Eastern neighbors, prefers the ethnic/religious model of self-definition to the territorial/political one. I would also point out that I consider one of the main causes for the breakup of Yugoslavia to be that the very vocal intellectuals representing minorities in the national bureaucracies abandoned the concept of a federative Yugoslav political nation in favor of one based not even on language but on criteria that are ethnic and religious. From the Yugoslav media that concept made its way to the West, which irresponsibly accepted the new priorities and the idea that the politicians espousing them could form nation-states along ethnic and religious lines without the agreement of the people involved. Everything that has happened in that unfortunate part of the world—all the murder, all the suffering—is intimately connected with the ideas of collective identity and nation espoused by the political class and with its ambition of that class to create unified, homogeneous states on the basis of ethnicity, religion, and language because that is what is good. Large multicolored states are bad; small solid-colored states are good.

True, Central Europe has a tendency to cleave to its ethnic and religious collective identity, but if we look at Northern Ireland, the Antwerp elections, or Italian separatism, if we consider that neo-Nazi views and neo-Nazi riots are no less prevalent in the western than in the eastern part of Germany, then we can state that the various parts of Europe are—to varying degrees—uncertain how to define *nation* and hence to determine exactly who belongs and who does not.

One advantage to European integration is that it cuts dilemmas like this one down to size. It obviates the necessity of children born of a mixed marriage choosing between mother and father, a situation deemed perfectly normal in the former Yugoslavia, where ethnicity (the last thing on the future parents' minds in their halcyon days of courtship) was of such vital importance to the state.

Another advantage to European integration is that it forces collective national identities—if only out of decency—to think of themselves in a broader framework, thereby attenuating their narcissism and fostering tolerance for a pluralist, multicultural ethos. Moreover, the logic of European integration encourages the territorial/political concept of the nation and the idea that the various linguistic and cultural communities—otherwise known as ethnic and religious entities—constitute valuable branches of the European nation.

European integration thus means that European Jews have every reason to stay where they are. If at the turn of the century and between the wars there was a middle class that dreamed of an integrated Europe, it was the Jewish middle class. Then came Hitler's New Europe and the Nuremberg Laws, and suddenly, by definition, Jews were no longer European.

The best thing, then, would be integration into Europe in the not too distant future. The next best thing would be integration within Central Europe. Much less satisfactory is the isolation complex: we are surrounded, we have no friends, or, even worse, we have only enemies. Such a scenario is unpleasant for the Jews, because it virtually requires the majority to define itself in ethnic and religious terms and view minorities as a fifth column. In an atmosphere of geopolitical neurosis it makes little practical difference what the minorities happen to be called—Jew or Hungarian, Serb or Croat, Muslim or Christian. Isolationism would be a great trial for any minority and could cause considerable emigration among the remaining Jews.

Despite the negative scenarios rehearsed here, I believe both pan-European integration and Central European integration are feasible and within reach. I believe that integration holds great possibilities for the inhabitants of the continent and that in a hopeful atmosphere, where much large-scale work remains to be done, Jews will be valued by their Christian neighbors as skilled and reliable partners.

If I place more credence in the positive scenario, it is partly out of habit—I regarded the Yalta-generated bloc system as a passing phantom long before others came to see it as such—and partly a consequence of my conviction that social and cultural processes (in the present instance, the growth of the middle class and cultural pluralism) exercise a broader, more decisive influence than the interests of one ideological wing of a national bureaucracy.

Having made the necessary exceptions (Bosnia and the Caucasus, areas of great chaos and new states, where demands for political autonomy by ethnic and religious communities have almost inevitably led to bloodshed), I would call East-Central Europe a basically stable part of the continent. Even if it has been going through the crisis that must accompany so radical a change in system, none of the West's subconscious fears of semibarbarian neighbors at the gates, none of the specters of mass migration, organized crime, and crazed extremism (to name but a few) have materialized dramatically. Czechoslovakia has split in two, but peacefully, and the rest of the countries are on a more or less even keel, managing to cope and accepting their national boundaries as they are. Securing civil rights for ethnic, cultural, religious, and linguistic minorities will take a long time, however, because it must be done in such a way as to avoid fanning the flames of secession and civil war among the majorities.

If fascism can be avoided, if we go on pretty much as we

have been going or perhaps ever so slightly better—in other words, if we have a state ruled by law, imperfect (even bumbling) yet dependable and democratic—then Jews have any number of alternatives open to them.

Hungary, for instance, has Jewish clubs, schools, journals, publishers. There are books on Jewish subjects in bookshop windows, programs about Jewish holidays on television. Judaism both as a religion and a universally accepted historical creed enjoys a certain legitimate respect. While many Jews here are not religious, many are—in their own way. Only a small percentage attend services and carry out the prescribed rituals.

There are quite a few Jews among liberal and socialist politicians and advisers, but there are also Jews among the conservatives. There are even some self-hating half- or three-quarter Jews on the staffs of radical right, anti-Semitic newspapers. Jews have made no special effort to organize as a national or ethnic minority; they have staked no claims for "positive discrimination," nor have they engaged in legislative lobbying: they represent too many points of view. The only political common denominator they have is the desire for democracy and basic human rights.

Neither assimilation nor dissimilation quite describes what is going on in the Jewish community. Both are taken seriously by its more thoughtful members, who do not wish to deny one identity for the sake of another. What a Jew writes is Jewish literature, but it can also be Hungarian or any other national literature.

People branded Jews by Nazi law can never forget that they are Jews: it is burned into their brains. But most Jews I know think of a Jew as a person who claims to be one—a claim non-Jews rarely make. If I think I am a Jew, then I am one, no matter where I am in the world, what clothes I wear, what customs I practice, even if I take into account the borders separating myself from the rest of the group, even if I do not solve the mystery of the world with the hypothesis of God.

1994

Hail and Farewell

The outgoing Parliament deserves our gratitude. You did a fine job, boys—each in your own way, each in your own role. The theater needs quaint types like you. Each of you had the good of the country at heart, each of you did what you could for it, according to your lights (and darks). You were good even when you were bad—working hard, doing your stuff, modest and proud, stimulating and stupid, witty and insipid.

For the time being all eyes are on Parliament. It is still our national arena, the place where many a stout lad and lass dream of standing next to the referee as he raises his or her right arm in the air. Blessed with natural vanity, they are out to win in the martial art known as politics.

But our politicians are applause-hungry actors as well: TV, radio, and newspaper actors who at the drop of a hat will stick out their chests in any room with long tables and people who have come to hear them (more than came when they weren't politicians and more than will come when they are politicians no more). They know how to adapt to their audiences. They have a daily, variable-length statement ready on demand. They turn on the minute they emerge from their cars and never say, "I couldn't possibly talk about that now" or "I have nothing pertinent to add." They have never dodged a question or a camera.

Our actors in the public interest deserve our gratitude for portraying the country's innermost thoughts and feelings through their own colorful characters, for showing us who we are and what we have to offer. Many people have their favorites among them, because many people—the old, the self-employed, the unemployed—sit and watch the gilded chamber day in and day out. Yesterday, when my mother happened to be watching, an attractive blond woman took the audience on a tour. "You wouldn't believe how clean it is, son. I wonder how many people it takes to keep a beautiful place like that spotless." It's the next best thing to being there.

Once I *was* there. In the gilded chamber. I spent an hour and a half listening to the debates, then thanked my friends the representatives for having got me a pass, wished them well, and skipped down the stairs and out of the building with the relief of a schoolboy playing truant. The rest of the boys were still up in their gaudy classroom, the teacher calling upon one or the other to recite.

Although I have had no desire to repeat my visit to the gilded chamber during these first four years, I am glad that from afar at least—walking along the embankment on the Buda side of the Danube or crossing Kossuth Square—I can respect the neo-Gothic gingerbread palace that in the old days, when my only use for it was the Parliamentary Library, I would tell naive tourists was a product of the fifteenth century (and they would believe me). I am glad that Parliament is not a mere tourist attraction, that things actually happen in the main chamber and backrooms and outbuildings. My sense of form is gratified by the knowledge that all party headquarters are in one place, that the president and the prime minister operate in close proximity, that the very geography of like-it-or-not communal living stimulates dialogue and works as a simple consensus-building technique against hard-nosed isolationism and for collegiality. I can testify to the fact that compromises among representatives of various party allegiances are perfectly possible, and I would claim that a culture of sober dialogue has developed as a result.

Daydreaming optimistically along these lines, I take a peep at the main chamber from my kitchen—by the good graces of the TV set in the corner—and nod to myself: yes, everyone is true to form. "You'll be out on your ear pretty soon," I think about some of them, occasionally wishing as much as thinking. In other words, the operation is proceeding smoothly. Most of the time I don't understand what they're talking about. I find that comforting.

But then a little fellow jumps up, calls me a traitor, and says I belong behind bars. My friends make fun of him, but that kind of attack is still possible. Then I spot the gloomy physiognomy of a former regular at our writers table. Clearly he hasn't got the thinly veiled Jew-baiting out of his system, and there he sits, bitter with frustration, thinking he'll probably have to table his hopes until 1998. I understand. Just as I understand censorship, breaking and entering, and homicide. They get my decent-citizen dander up, and I don't calm down until I stop understanding again. Then I turn off the set. I can do without it, though I like to think of myself as a responsible citizen.

I would like us to have a civilized political class aware of the respect due the citizen, that is, exhibiting the most rudimentary forms of human accountability. I do not like being called a traitor. In a gilded chamber or any other. As long as that sort of thing is possible, the language of politics will grate on my ears and we shall have no such thing as an accountable—subject to proper civil jurisdiction—class of politicians.

I tell everyone (no matter what language is coming at me from the other end of the camera) what I think. I called censorship censorship in the former regime, and I call it censorship in this one. The politicians involved can indict me and recommend the stiffest sentence in the land if they please. I'm surprised at the way their minds work. It's all so déjà vu. Once they called me an agent of imperialism. That's what you were if you said that two times two is four. I would think we were back where we started if I didn't throw an occasional glance at the calendar.

This sort of thing is still possible, perfectly normal, quite common actually. My friends laugh it off, but I tell reporters, "Once a fool, always a fool." An elderly woman with dyed hair hisses "Shame!" as she passes me in the street. The disingenuous picture-box is full of language like that, coupling it week after week with my photograph. There's no ban on humor, after all. The sanctioned kind.

I see angry, indignant looks coming at me. "Look at him," they say, "out for a stroll." What have I done this time? Some proffer friendly words and—as during the former regime—hurry on, looking this way and that. I get anonymous phone calls from people calling me dirty rat, dirty bastard, dirty Jew, predicting I'll die like a dog, forgetting that they too are mortal.

The most venomous are my coevals, people who were furious with me when I was banned and who are now doing the banning. If I feel like turning off the set, it's because I don't want to hear their grunts coming from the nation's gilded chamber, the political nation's schoolroom. I'd rather hear something I don't understand, something I can fall asleep to with my heart at peace.

It is heartening to know that a professional political class which accepts all players as legitimate has sprung up. The men and women who have been elected are our legitimate representatives, and most of them have learned a great deal during these past four years. A goodly percentage of them will doubtless be returning for the next act. But the time has come for a weeding-out process in which every voter can have a say. Since many people are bitter, passions are running high, and the pendulum of emotion is unlikely to stop, both the theater company and its acting style are bound to change noticeably.

I hope that expertise, experience, and proximity to a civilized, international level of political discourse will come to be prerequisites for membership in our political class and that in all parties and election districts they will constitute the leading issues. And while it is clear that in politics at least the brightest and best rarely make it to the top, we can breathe easy if roughly the brightest and relatively the best end up there. Then we can do our jobs and leave them to do theirs; then politics is a service and politicians and the law-abiding citizen's servants, bound and beholden to respect both the citizen and the autonomy of civic society and forbidden to threaten, intimidate, or brainwash any member of that society.

What we need—and it appears to be taking shape—is a book of etiquette indicating how far members of Parliament may go, where the line must be drawn. Scandalmongers are entertaining and may hold center stage for a while, but they soon grow into superannuated, self-parodying clowns. How do they work? By attacking an entire group, by maligning it in such a way as to acquire notoriety, by dipping into the stock of ready-made moral and political rhetoric that makes their hatred sound righteous. The gilded chamber is a perfect opportunity for all sorts of high-caliber Tartuffes, and if they fall on their face, well, it's all part of the game.

As I say, it's heartening to know we have developed a political class. And a constitution and rules of the game. I see intelligent laws being proposed and attractive, thinking people debating them. But I also see how a few cheap tricks can mangle the constitution or the press, and I realize I find so much heartening that I forget to be disheartened by how little reassuring experience I have had with Hungarian governments from Gömbös to Boross, the only exceptions being Ferenc Nagy and Imre Nagy, who might have been decent rulers but had only flash-in-the-pan kingdoms to rule.

József Antall's government might have been decent if it had joined forces with the opposition roundtable, but instead of the country before his eyes he saw a country he had made up, and when it failed to resemble him, he branded it morally wrong. In other words, the first democratically elected prime minister to serve out his term saw himself, much as his predecessors did, standing above the country, and if he gave in all too readily to the temptation to expand his sphere of influence and determine the direction of culture and public discourse, he did so because he considered the style of Horthy-era paternalism (as opposed to Kádár-era paternalism) a kind of family heritage and chose to follow it, with some emendations and updating, in the interest of historical continuity.

Thus the Kádár ethos that permeated society for so long gave way to an attempt at revitalizing the Horthy ethos, though of course the people involved in the switch had been involved up to their ears in the Kádár ethos and gave few signs of wishing to extricate themselves from it. Besides, both societies were marked by censorship, a legacy not easily thrown off. The elites of both accepted the advantages of that legacy—its anecdotes, memories, schools, connections, and the goods and property that followed therefrom. They must now be willing to accept the bad conscience that is part and parcel of it as well.

Nor can the untested newcomers be particularly sure of themselves: no government in power is above reproach. We can all find reasons to be ashamed of ourselves if the mood comes upon us. Horrendous crimes have been committed here in the name of the radical right *and* the radical left.

There was and is an audience for aggressive rhetoric—who the villains are, who is to blame, who needs to be done in— but never too large an audience. Clearly most people want the center to do the governing. What they do not want is for political reliability to prevail again over expertise, for officials and party bureaucrats to lord it over the intelligentsia.

When Antall came to power, the country did not consist of two democratic teams—or even one, for that matter—yet he had no interest in a coalition. Broadly based centrist co-alitions are called for in critical situations—when, for instance, moral authority based on the authority of power is being re-placed by a new republic. Antall's lineup did scant honor to the name of politician.

Governmental politics is a closed affair aimed primarily at the opposition, and by acting hurt and suspicious and reviving the policy of a one-party system it made the opposition out to be demonic. Moreover, since the arrogance of power precluded all natural dialogue, there could be no easygoing, matter-of-fact give and take, and communist mythology was replaced by a new mythology rather than by genuine Hungarian culture. All this has hindered creative elements from combining forces and has surely done the country great moral and material harm.

Civil servants have swollen into missionaries. People who claim that nothing can happen without them and that history has sent them to fulfill a mission should fail the civil service examination. The new political class must learn humility. What we want from politicians is clarity, not didactic rhetoric. If only we could disqualify from politics anyone who has at any time or in any circumstance proved a liar. If only the electorate would realize that lying is a recurrent vice.

A political class deserves neither exceptional respect nor exceptional contempt. If politicians assume too much responsibility, if society raises them to the status of paternalistic figures, then it will applaud them even as it topples them for failing—as fail they must—to meet its expectations. Then both victory and defeat are more existential, if not more hysterical, than they need be. If a political class acts on its own, the government will swell.

But if we have a strong, enterprising population and a strong, educated middle class, if we have self-respecting social and professional organizations, and if the nonstate sector takes root and formulates a set of clear-cut desiderata, then the government will never dream of expanding in the direction of a dictatorship—or if it does, it will immediately be taken to account.

The formation of a middle class was the most interesting social development of the eighties. The change in regime has only intensified the process, and by the end of this decade we shall be a more or less normal bourgeois society. The process of *embourgeoisement* is stronger than any political ideology, stronger than state socialism or state nationalism. People wishing to play an ongoing role in our government must be committed to a continuation of that process based on a dialogue with the population.

If Hungarian democracy is to make a valid response to the issues facing us at the end of the century, we must call for moderation from our political class. We must take a long, hard look at the two legacies of our century—the Horthy period and the Kádár period, the gentry tradition and the feudal-bureaucratic tradition—which are amazingly similar. (Both, for example, granted the politician a hegemonic position.) And while both have failed, their traditions live on in the personalities—and children—of their followers and are seeking an outlet.

Now that the Hungarian political class has had the experience of losing—and losing is an experience it will inevitably continue having—it must master the art of being a *good* loser. In politics as in cards there is little point in ranting and raving. There are waves, there are winning streaks. Politics is as unpredictable as the hit parade or the bestseller list.

It cannot be denied: the mighty are falling. Up they go, up and up, and just as they think they've reached the top and start strutting and crowing, people turn against them. Good, plain reliability, then, is a worthy investment. Why should we expect more from a politician than we do from a scientist or judge?

First the pendulum swung to the right; now it is swinging to the left. But we would be unwise to forget that the pendulum is constantly in motion and that what we need throughout the to-ing and fro-ing the great parade of rhetoric, is a center capable of dialogue and consensus. As long as things are more or less under control, the choices facing the voter are not all that dramatic. There will be one or two dramas before we reach nirvana, but nirvana, too, is only temporary.

1994

Translator's Afterword

"Long live György Konrád, the greatest Hungarian writer!" a demonstrator shouts. "But not too long."

Konrád tells the story of the demonstration in "15 March: A Colorful Day" with the understatement characteristic of much of this collection. The subject matter itself is nothing if not drastic, but Konrád refuses to be thrown by it. His equanimity is due in part to knowing exactly where he stands on the issues at hand, and his stand comes from what can only be called an unfashionably moral anchor. Resolutely postmodern in the way his novels combine history, autobiography, and fiction, he refuses to accept postmodernism's moral relativity. As he states unequivocally and in numerous contexts: Thou shalt not kill.

Not surprisingly, Konrád shares the belief in moral absolutes with his Czech compatriot in dissidence, Václav Havel. Both are exemplary Central European writers who could not emerge into active public life—into history, as it were—until their respective countries had emerged from years of totalitarian stalemate; both have chosen to put their artistic lives temporarily on hold. But while Havel has accepted political office, Konrád clings to the role of intellectual gadfly. True to the concept of oppositional activism he set forth in his *Antipolitics*, he has spent much of his time lecturing at local, national, and international forums and producing a steady stream of essays.

The period he writes about in this collection was characterized by a swing away from the militantly internationalist stance imposed by the communist regimes to an equally militant nationalist stance. Konrád, having barely escaped death in the Holocaust and living in a country that borders on the former Yugoslavia, is understandably sensitive to the plight of ethnic minorities under attack. When the Hungarians allowed the East Germans to cross their border into Austria, thereby starting the domino effect that culminated in the collapse of the Iron Curtain, he traveled to the Berlin Wall to give a speech ("Thoughts on the Border") hailing the breakdown of borders in general.

Konrád's aversion to borders and the collective identities they engender naturally leads him to an interest in the European Union and, by extension, any supranational construct. Significantly, his thoughts on the Hungarian national character ("Being Hungarian in Europe," "What Makes a Hungarian?") place nationality in a pan-European context. And if nationalism cannot be entirely dispensed with, he calls for a non-militant nationalism. Why not take pride, for example, in one's own individual contribution to the nation or in a figure like the mid-nineteenth-century poet Petőfi, whose poetry and politics brought Hungary "into Europe" and thus served as a force for integration.

The comeback made in the early eighties by the idea of a

supranational Central Europe as a means of differentiating the East bloc from the Soviet Union lost steam as the Soviet Union lost power. By the late eighties many of the ideas's proponents had taken to identifying with Western Europe. Not so Konrád. He evokes numerous historical and cultural features shared by the countries of Central Europe. Yet he does so not out of nostalgia. On an abstract level he is reacting against the east-west polarization of recent memory and against any bi-polar model that is cast as a struggle between good (us) versus evil (them). But his reasons for keeping the Central European alternative alive are also pragmatic given the ethnically mixed and potentially explosive populations along the borders of the nation-states in the region, a historically and culturally justified geopolitical framework of the sort might well help to defuse the borders and mitigate fundamentalist, tribalistic animosities ("Identity and Hysteria," "Dematerializing Borders," "Central Europe Redivivus," "Eternally Waiting").

Crucial to all Konrád's deliberations on ethnicity is the role played by civil rights and a civil society. Rejecting both the has-been state socialism developed by Communist regimes and the would-be state nationalism of certain successor regimes, he continually reaffirms his faith in what used to be denigrated as "bourgeois democracy"; in fact, he measures the progress of Central Europe in general—and Hungary in particular—the return of the middle class and of rule by law ("A New Year's Prediction for 1990," "Revolution or Reform"). He is thus chronicling the tongue-in-cheek definition of socialism, circa 1989: a painful stage on the path from capitalism to capitalism.

If Konrád admires the middle class, he does so less for its ability to produce or consume than for its espousal of liberal, democratic values: he often qualifies the term "middle class" with the adjective "educated." And although he clearly prefers its Anglo-American variety, he is not entirely uncritical of it. During a teaching stint in America during the mid-eighties he bemoaned the lack of dissidence in American public life, noting that the country had many university teachers but few intellectuals.

Several esays deal with the Democratic Charter, the organization Konrád spearheaded to involve more citizens in the democratic process ("What Is the Charter?," "Being a Citizen," "The Holiday Looks Back"). While conceiving the Charter as a grassroots organization, he is also passionately concerned with the place of his fellow intellectuals in the new order. In 1977 he and a colleague, Iván Szelényi, went to prison for writing *Intellectuals on the Road to Class Power,* a study that exposed the complicity of the Hungarian intelligentsia with the postwar regime. To avoid falling into the power trap this time around, Konrád suggests, intellectuals must exploit their freedom to the hilt and assert their individualities ("More than Nothing: The Role of the Intellectual in a Changing Europe").

As a novelist, Konrád is even more passionately concerned with writers ("Something Is Over," "Hedonists of the Brain"), but his concern is far from narcissistic. It stems instead from a belief in literature—and, more specifically, in Goethe's "world literature"—as a major humanizing force. He goes so far as to call literature the "legal code of our humanism," the foundation for the "self-awareness of our civil society."

What holds the world together? he asks, and answers: "Consensus, constitutions, the rules of the game . . . And, I might add, literature. Its works, its knowledge, its memory." Art is the "only proper place for anarchy": art is a place where "killing is depicted rather than enacted." Art transcends borders: "The symbols basic to the system of relationships we live by come to us through literature; literature enables us to slip into the skin of humanity."

Why then should "the greatest Hungarian writer" temporarily abandon fiction and turn to the essay? The most obvious answer is that external events proved so compelling they virtually forced the essay form upon him. But there is another factor: Konrád finds borders suspect in literature as in geography; he thus leaves the boundary between novel and essay purposely hazy.

Konrád came to write his first novel while a social worker. He belongs to the uniquely Hungarian school of fiction that emerged in the inter-war period and was known as "sociography," a consciously reality-based strain of novel-writing that bears comparison with the works of, say, Dreiser and Dos Passos. Moreover, Central European writers from Broch and Musil to Kundera make a practice of incorporating essays into their fiction.

But the roots of Konrád's essays go back farther, to the roots of the essay itself and Montaigne. In Konrád as in Montaigne the essay is an "assay," an attempt at working out an idea or personal experience. The current selection, which encompasses approximately a tenth of his post-communist essays, includes representative examples of speeches and lectures, homilies ("The Meek Shall Inherit the Earth"), letters to the editor, meditations, aphorisms ("To Hungarian Serbs and Croats"), and diary entries ("Snapshot on the Day After All Saints' Day"); they show him accepting awards from heads of state and giving birthday parties for his young sons. Like Montaigne, Konrád combines compassion with skepticism: his counterpart to Montaigne's famous motto, "Que sçay-je?" (What know I?), is the remark that literature takes us beyond the naive question of who is right.

What is right—what is morally tenable—is another question. Literature can suggest answers, but is by its nature too ironic to serve as a court of last resort. Konrád therefore goes one step further—to the Judeo-Christian tradition, where he finds "Thou shalt not kill," and "Love your enemies."

In a different context Konrád restates the latter as follows: "Neither a normal person nor a normal nation has enemies." Here, as throughout the essays, Konrád juxtaposes public morality and private morality, insisting that in a civil society the two should support each other. No wonder he cautions against expecting too much from politicians.

Konrád's standards are the highest. In the mordant essay that concludes the volume he finds the first post-communist government severely wanting ("Hail and Farewell"), yet maintains a guarded—melancholic, if you like—optimism. Rebirth there most definitely is. A civil society, however imperfect, is still in place.

Los Angeles, 1994